"Susan and Laura Stachler's story is as heartwarming as a plate of warm cookies. More than a cancer survival story, this is the beautiful tale of two tough cookies who built a successful business on grit, determination, and love. I was rooting for them both, and you will too."

—Teresa J. Rhyne, #1 *New York Times*
bestselling author

"This mother-daughter duo's story of courage and love is inspirational. Susan's one tough cookie and her mom's got chutzpah! I found *The Cookie Cure* to be an entertaining and heartfelt read."

—Ethan Zohn, reality TV personality
and cofounder of Grassroot Soccer

"Susan and Laura Stachler's story is an incredible journey that truly shows what's possible—how a mother-daughter team can band together to stare cancer in the face, heal, and put true sweetness in the world. It's about not letting heartbreaking loss define your future. The Stachlers show you can take the hardest of times, turn your struggles inside out, and find your true purpose. *The Cookie Cure* is sure to inspire many who are facing devastating times to see the possibility of a sweeter future ahead."

—Daryn Kagan, former CNN anchor
and author of *Hope Possible*

"I quickly discovered there's nothing cookie-cutter about Susan and Laura's story. Inspiring, moving, and surprising all at once: *The Cookie Cure* will make you feel warm all over."

—Mark Strassmann, CBS News Correspondent

"You want inspiration? Meet Susan, who fought cancer and built a family business with her mom at the same time. From the moment I met Susan and her mother I felt a kinship with them. Starting a family business was one of the toughest experiences I've lived through. But, to read the story of Susan battling a life-threatening illness and together with her mom creating Susansnaps? Wow. So meet Susan and get inspired. People all over this country will connect with her story. *The Cookie Cure* is long overdue."

—Jamie Deen, American cook, restaurateur, and author of *Jamie Deen's Good Food*

"The story shared by these real-life steel magnolias is a true testament to their grace, strength, and resilience."

—Lisa Frederick, editor in chief, *Southern Lady* magazine

"Occasionally in life, we will meet someone who will inspire us in many ways. Susan is one of those people. If the world had more people like Susan in it, it would be a better place."

—Ron Gant, former Major League Baseball player and Anchor of Fox5 *Good Day Atlanta*

THE COOKIE CURE

the COOKIE CURE

A MOTHER · DAUGHTER MEMOIR
OF COOKIES AND CANCER

Susan Stachler
with Laura Stachler

sourcebooks

Published by Sourcebooks, Inc.
P.O. Box 4410, Naperville, Illinois 60567-4410
(630) 961-3900
Fax: (630) 961-2168
sourcebooks.com

Library of Congress Cataloging-in-Publication Data

Names: Stachler, Susan, author. | Stachler, Laura, author.
Title: The cookie cure : a mother/daughter memoir of cookies and cancer / Susan and Laura Stachler.
Description: Naperville, Illinois : Sourcebooks, [2018]
Identifiers: LCCN 2017030949 |
Subjects: LCSH: Stachler, Susan--Health. | Cancer--Patients--United States--Biography. | Businesswomen--United States--Biography. | Cookie industry--United States. | Mothers and daughters--United States.
Classification: LCC RC265.6.S73 A3 2018 | DDC 362.19699/40092 [B] --dc23 LC record available at https://lccn.loc.gov/2017030949

Printed and bound in the United States of America.
VP 10 9 8 7 6 5 4 3 2 1

If ever there is tomorrow when we're not together...there is something you must always remember. You are braver than you believe, stronger than you seem, and smarter than you think. But the most important thing is, even if we're apart... I'll always be with you.

—A. A. Milne

Contents

Dear Sue,

I didn't know you were terminal until you were dead.

Mother and Dad raised us in a fun, loving home. You were my big sister, four years older than me, and we were inseparable. Our time together was filled with the normal things sisters do—shopping for clothes at Judy's, learning how to play guitar, squeezing lemon juice on our hair to turn it blond, laying our freckled bodies out to try to get a sunny Southern California tan, watching Johnny Carson, and eating midnight snacks. And there was something else, something that somehow seemed normal at the time. You went to the doctor every three weeks.

How did I not know?

It all started one night when we went to Shakey's Pizza with the rest of the family. We were all chatting, waiting for our pizza to arrive, when you said, "Daddy, I have something right here…" and rubbed your shoulder. And what did I think? Nothing. I was only ten. You were fourteen. But for some reason, I remember that moment very clearly. You went to see Dr. Swift, our pediatrician, and soon after, you went to the hospital for surgery. Mother and Dad bought a second TV and put it in my bedroom "for anyone in the family who happens to get sick." The doctor told them you had Stage 4 Hodgkin's disease—a blood cancer that affects lymph nodes—but they didn't tell me about your diagnosis. They didn't even tell you the full story.

Years after your death, they told me the doctors had given you three years to live and said you would not graduate from high school. I realize now how lucky we were—you lived eleven years longer than the doctors predicted you would. At the time, Mother and Dad simply told you that you had a blood disorder; they never said the word cancer. *It was 1963, a different time. Now, everyone knows everything about everything. Instead of* Webster's Dictionary, *we use* Google. *I carry a little device, about the size of a deck of cards, in my hand, and it can give me the answers to any question I have. Mother and Dad decided to protect you by not telling you everything. And you went to the doctor every three weeks for a checkup. It became a part of who you were, just something you did.*

If Mother and Dad had told you that you only had three years to live, would you have been waiting to die? What if they had told you in the beginning, when you still felt well, that you had a limited amount of time left? You wouldn't have been the same. Instead, we lived our lives, you went to the doctor every few weeks, and I didn't even realize how sick you were. At least, not until you came to visit me during my freshman year of college.

I was so thrilled that everyone in the dorm would see me going out that night with my cool older sister. I was getting ready in my small, shared dorm room when the door flew open. You entered, gasping for air. Immediately, I turned to the rotary phone behind me and called the operator. "I have an emergency! My sister's here, and she can't breathe. She's not breathing. I'm in the dorm on the third floor, USC campus." You slid down from the edge of the bed onto the floor, slumped over. I rushed to you, shouting, "Sue, what's wrong?" You couldn't answer. You were still gasping, your head tilted back as you tried to suck in air. I went back to the phone and yelled into the receiver, "Please hurry! I need help!" I didn't know what to do.

I ran into the hall, screaming, "Can someone help me?" It was early in the school year, and I didn't know anyone on my floor yet. One, two, three doors down I found help. A girl hurriedly followed me back and helped me get you onto the bed. By then your mouth was clenched shut and your body was rigid. I didn't know what was happening. Kneeling next to you on the bed, I sobbed as I wrapped my arms around you. I thought you were dying right there in my arms.

Finally, the paramedics arrived. As they got into position to help you, one asked, "What happened here?"

All I knew to say was, "My sister has Hodgkin's disease."

Years later, after we both were married, I lived for our ridiculously long, twice-weekly phone calls. I was perplexed one Saturday when you couldn't come to the phone. Hoxsie went to tell you I was calling but quickly got back on the line and said you wouldn't be able to talk to me. He didn't sound like himself.

A day later I got a call from Dad. "Laura, I'm calling from the hospital in Palm Springs. Your mother and I are here with Sue. You need to come as soon as you can. We are waiting with Hoxsie. Your sister is not doing well."

Before I hung up the phone, I said, "You know I'll be there as soon as I can. But, Dad, I can't go in. I can't see her this time." I couldn't bear the thought of you being sick again. My voice broke. "I can't, Dad."

You know Dad, calm and understanding. He just said, "Okay, honey, you just need to get here."

When I arrived at the hospital, of course I went in to see you. I was terrified, but I walked into your hospital room. You were resting, your eyes closed.

"Sue."

You blinked when I said your name and tried to look my way.

"Sue, it's me. It's Laura," I said. "I'm right here. You're doing such a good job. Everyone here is so nice, and they're taking good care of you." When I reached over the side rail of the bed and slid my hand into yours, I felt you squeeze my fingers. I blinked back tears, not wanting you to see how scared I was. "You're doing such a good job. Please keep trying."

I didn't know if you had any strength left, but what if all you needed to help you get through this was for me to push you one more time? Did you hear me when I told you my plan?

"Ken and I have already talked about it. When you go home, I'm coming to stay with you 'til you get better."

Your calmness frightened me. You already knew, didn't you? We would never see each other again.

When your hand released mine, Dad said, "Sue, you get some rest, sweetie. Why don't you sleep a little?"

My heart started to race. You looked so tired but peaceful. I was shattered. I didn't know what to think, wasn't sure what was happening. All I knew was that you were very, very sick. As Dad stepped away from the side of your bed, he touched my arm, signaling it was time to go. I leaned over you. Could you hear me? "I know we never had to say this to each other," I said, "but I love you." I moved up to your forehead and kissed you. "I'm not leaving you," I promised. "I'll be right outside, and I'll see you soon."

I remember driving away from the hospital hours later, looking at the people in their cars going past. They didn't even know what had just happened. You were gone.

My Name Is Susan

ISN'T IT FUNNY THAT FROM THE TIME WE'RE BORN, we each respond to a name, our very own name? When you think about it, a name is just some letters and sounds put together, but it becomes our identity—who we are. It's the first thing people learn about us ("Hi! My name is..."), and it's stuck with us forever.

I got lucky. I like my name. I always have. Classic, simple: Susan. I'm named for my aunt Susan. I hear she was quite amazing, and I've always felt that being associated with her, purely through this five-letter name my parents bestowed upon me, makes me pretty special. That's how it works, right? My aunt and me. Two girls, one name. We never met, but we have a bond that lasts forever.

Growing up, my ears would perk up at the slightest mention of Aunt Sue. I wanted to know more about this person: the other Susan, the original Susan. My aunt died before I was born, when she was twenty-eight. I came along four years later. It wasn't like Mom went around talking about her sister all the time. But when she did, it was never so much *what* she said that drew me in, but *how* she said it. I grew to love Aunt Sue because Mom loved her, and I loved my mom. I took it upon myself to be the best Susan possible. I thought if Mom saw a glimmer of her sister in me, maybe, just maybe, she'd miss her a little bit less.

I constantly put pressure on myself to do things right. I took on having this name just like I do everything else—with full-on commitment—and the stress I sometimes feel about it is honestly a bit ridiculous. It's not always easy being me. For some reason, even things that don't matter in the big picture matter to me. Decisions as simple as whether to have M&M'S or Skittles for a movie snack or what appetizer to make for a family dinner have been known to put me in a quandary. I can't help myself. I wish I could. But striving for my best works for me. So I've always wanted to get "being Susan" right.

I'm one of four kids. We're boy, girl, boy, girl, and I'm number two. Mom says, "We all come with a thumbprint," and mine has a definite pattern of control and organization. I plan, take charge, direct, sort out, and put things in order. I want things to be black and white. I like to know the end of the movie first, and I read the last page of a book before I begin chapter one. It might sound boring to some people, but I like to know what's coming.

Ever since my first day of kindergarten, when I confidently

announced to my class, "Hi! My name is Susan. I'm named for my aunt Sue," I've liked school. Maybe it's because I like structure and rules and following along. Go to class, take notes, take a test, then on to the next one. In elementary school, I was already setting goals for graduating high school and getting into a good college. The next thing I knew, I was twenty-two years old, a senior majoring in communication at Auburn University, and my school days were coming to an end. My diploma, my ticket to the outside world, would be in my hands in a matter of months.

Putting pressure on myself to do well in school was one thing, but I took it to a new level when I started off my senior year of college by buying a suit, walking it into my newly rented apartment, and hanging it in my closet. It was a traditional, jet-black, two-piece skirt suit with coordinating black leather heels. This would be my interview suit, and it would land me a job. I had no idea what kind of job I would get or even what I wanted to do, but I knew if the interview required me to wear a suit and heels, that would be a good start. Every day, as I pulled on jeans and a T-shirt, ready to zip off to class, I'd eye that suit. It was a constant reminder: *stay focused*.

In order to get a chance to wear that suit, I'd need a strong résumé. My experience as a server in a Mexican restaurant and a barbecue joint, with one summer of office-temp work mixed in, wasn't going to be much help in the corporate world. As the weeks went by and I worried, *What am I going to do to fill in the white space?* I found myself working to keep my GPA up, piling on campus activities, and even volunteering for Relay For Life, a fund-raising event. Solid plan.

There was also something else going on in my life. One day after New Year's, while I was still home on break, I heard the back door slam shut in the middle of the afternoon. My mom called out, "Ken, is that you? You okay?"

Dad answered with a resounding no. It was the first and only time I had ever heard my dad say he wasn't okay. He had lost his job, and at the worst possible time. He'd been battling cancer and was still undergoing chemotherapy, and, meanwhile, Mom had been talking about taking action on one of her dreams: starting a bakery out of our house. I wished there was something I could do to help, but all I could do was go back to school, study hard, interview for jobs, and start a career. My parents gave me everything I ever needed—and a lot of what I wanted—and I couldn't wait to call home and say, *Mom and Dad, I have a job! Now there's one less person for you to worry about.*

As spring break approached, I looked forward to a week of hanging out at home and not really doing anything. Auburn University is in Alabama, a two-hour drive from our house in Atlanta. My friends were either going to the beach or on a cruise, but I was happy to head home. There had been a lot going on with my family, so I thought it would be nice to spend some time with them.

My boyfriend, Randy, came home with me for a couple of days too. We had met at Auburn three years earlier and become best friends. He somehow managed to be the life of the party while at the same time keeping to himself, his nose in a book. He was born in Mississippi but had grown up in small towns in Louisiana, and he was a rugged guy with a baby face—totally intriguing. Luckily, my family loved him too, and he was always welcome at our house.

After dinner one night, as we were hanging out in the family room, Mom casually said to me, "Don't forget you have a doctor's appointment tomorrow."

"What?" I shouldn't have been surprised—Mom was always sneaking up on us with doctor's appointments.

Mom said, "Yes, a checkup, and I got you in with the dentist on Wednesday."

"The dentist too?" I was not pleased. I hated going to the doctor. The dentist was no better; actually, it was way worse. No matter how much I brushed and flossed, I still got cavities. I quickly gave my litany of reasons why I didn't need to go to either appointment.

Mom just laughed. "Okay. Pick one."

The next morning as I tried to leave for the doctor, I couldn't keep my car from rolling down the steep angle of our driveway, and I got stuck. It was a stick shift, and I wasn't good at driving it. Pressed for time, I had no choice but to get Randy so he could drive me. As I sat beside him in the waiting room, I felt self-conscious—it wasn't exactly cool to drag your boyfriend along to your doctor's appointment. Soon, the door opened and a nurse peered into the waiting room. "Susan?"

"Sorry about this," I said to Randy. "I'll be right back."

I stepped on the scale, changed into the paper gown, and sat patiently as the nurse practitioner checked me over. I figured it was about time for her to be through, but she kept running her fingertips up and down, side to side, along my neck and over my collarbone. Again, up and down, side to side.

"Susan, have you ever felt anything here?" she asked.

I stiffened. "No."

Still pressing her fingers along the base of my neck, she asked, "Have you noticed anything unusual?"

Again, I answered, "No." I had no idea what she was talking about.

"Okay," she responded. "I'd like to get the doctor to take a second look. I'll be right back."

Once the door had closed behind her, I too began to do the finger dance across my neck. As my fingertips reached a hard, round protrusion sticking out behind the top of my collarbone, I gasped. *She was right. There is something.* It felt like the top of an apricot was stuck under the surface of my skin. *How did I not notice this? I notice everything down to each new freckle I get, so how did I not feel this?*

In a matter of minutes, our family doctor, Dr. Seyfried,

came into the room and moved his fingers thoroughly along my neck. I was starting to get upset, but I was trying with all my might to stay calm. I simply sat there, watching his every facial expression, waiting for any indication of what might be going on. "Have you been sick or tired or noticed any weight gain or loss?" he asked. "Have you felt this?"

"No," I said again, reluctantly.

I began second-guessing myself as my mind kept racing, wondering how I hadn't noticed this thing first and what it could possibly be.

Finally, Dr. Seyfried said, "I believe there may be an issue with your thyroid."

All I could think was, *My thyroid? Doesn't that mean weight gain?*

"Let's run some blood work, get you in for an ultrasound," he said.

I was still stuck on *I don't want to blow up.* Keeping my absurd thoughts to myself, I timidly mustered, "What does this mean?"

He answered assuredly, "Thyroid problems are common and easily managed. Don't get ahead of yourself. If there is an issue, we can treat it."

Tears were building behind my eyes. That was easy for him to say. He was a health-conscious, fit, middle-aged, married man with three kids. I was a twenty-two-year-old girl. He could afford to gain pounds; I couldn't, or so I thought.

Dr. Seyfried didn't have clear answers, and that left me uneasy. By the time I came out to the waiting room, I was flustered. Randy's not one to rehash things, so once he'd said, "Don't worry. You're fine," we didn't talk about it anymore. We went off to lunch, although I didn't feel much like eating, and spent the afternoon out and about. But I couldn't keep myself from constantly reaching up and touching my neck. Now that I knew the lump was there, I couldn't stop thinking about it.

When we got home, my parents were doing some gardening in the backyard. Without hesitating, I walked over to Mom and blurted out, "There's something wrong with me."

She set her rake aside and turned to me. "All right. What's wrong?"

"I need your hand," I said. "Give me your hand."

After she yanked off her gardening glove, I pressed Mom's left hand to the bulge in my neck. I waited to see her initial reaction. A forced smile broke across her face as her nostrils flared and her eyes got big. It was her classic "I'm staying calm, but I'm concerned" look.

Mom called out, "Ken, can you come here?" I didn't want to make a big deal out of it, but it was too late. Dad put down his shovel, walked around the pool, and met us on the patio.

"Did Dr. Seyfried feel this?" Mom asked. "What did he say? Should I call him?"

Frustrated and confused, I pulled away. "He thinks I have

some kind of thyroid problem or something. I don't know. I have to go for an ultrasound next week."

As Mom continued to examine my neck, I tried to tell her again what the doctor had said, but she wasn't listening. She stood there looking unsure while she attempted to calm me down. "Okay, I'm sorry I wasn't there. I'm sure it's nothing. You're fine, Susan."

That was exactly what I wanted to hear and what I knew she would say. I knew she would listen to me. I knew she would care, and I knew she'd tell me to not worry. But, looking back now, I realize how insensitive I was. I wanted Mom to comfort me about the lump, but I didn't even think about how she would feel when I put her fingers to my throat. I temporarily forgot that she is terrified of hearing anyone say, "Can you feel this?" I can't blame her. After all, Mom's sister, one of her favorite people, died from lumps in her throat, neck, and chest. I also knew the more recent story of how Mom woke up one morning to find Dad rubbing his throat. Lying in bed with his head tilted back on the pillow, he took Mom's hand and asked, "What is this?" as he rubbed her fingers along a golf ball–size lump under his chin. At first his doctor thought it was part of a persistent cold, but it too turned out to be cancer. So, no. Mom doesn't like lumps.

Mom and Dad were forty-one when Dad's "bad cold" was diagnosed as non-Hodgkin's lymphoma. I was thirteen at the time and didn't understand a whole lot about the disease, which is how my parents wanted it. They told my brothers, my sister, and me at dinner one night. They carefully played it off as if they were saying, *Dad has brown hair and wears glasses*, but they were actually saying, "Dad has cancer. It's called non-Hodgkin's lymphoma. It's a type of blood cancer that affects the lymph nodes and immune system. He has a very good doctor, and all will be well." I later learned that at his first appointment, his oncologist, Dr. Weens, told my parents that Dad's cancer was incurable.

As I stood on the patio with my parents staring at my throat, all I wanted was for the random thing in my neck to disappear. We didn't need it. Not me and especially not my parents. Dad was home during the week looking for a new finance position and gardening, and Mom had bakery equipment being installed in the garage, of all places, in a couple of weeks. None of that was normal. I was also concerned because our health insurance through Dad's former employer was about to run out. *Is an ultrasound necessary? How much will it cost?* No. I just wanted the stupid lump to go away. Couldn't I even do a simple checkup "right"?

Dear Sue,

Less than an hour after you died, Mother turned to me and said, "I hope, if you have a daughter one day, you'll name her Susan." In that moment, I didn't think she was giving me permission to use your name; I thought she meant it more as, Where one life ends, maybe another will carry on. *In her anguish, somehow, she saw hope. I certainly wouldn't have needed any prompting to use your name, but four years later, when Ken and I had our first daughter, it was nice to know I already had Mother's blessing. It would be no surprise for Dad and her to hear that we'd named our baby girl for you.*

2

Oh, To Be Tested

SPRING BREAK WAS OVER, CLASSES HAD RESUMED, and I was lying flat on my back on a vinyl examination table in the middle of a dark room waiting for my ultrasound to begin. While two technicians hovered over me, setting up the equipment, I quietly settled in. In a matter of minutes, their metal wand would produce some images on a screen, giving us the answer to what lay beneath my skin, and the waiting and wondering would be over. I felt calmer than I had in days.

The technicians were whispering softly to each other as they got the computer situated. Finally, one of the women went to her desk in the corner while the other said, "I'm sorry for the wait."

"Oh, it's fine. I'm good."

She squeezed some clear, thick jelly on the end of the metal wand. "This will be cold." She placed the gooey end of the wand under my chin and began slowly sliding it down my neck, then, little by little, inching it back up.

I turned my head to watch the monitor. It showed gray, white, and black blurry images that meant nothing to me. I have no idea what I thought I was going to see or decipher, but I still looked. I wanted to see. I wanted to know.

The technician continued to massage my neck with the wand, and the test seemed to be going smoothly. Earlier, in the waiting room, Mom had told me, "Be thinking about what you'd like for lunch. When you're done, we'll go wherever you'd like." So, I was thinking, *Should we order cheese dip or guacamole?*

My thoughts came to a halt when the tech lifted the wand and said, "Can you tell me exactly what is wrong?"

Politely, but quizzically, I said, "I was told there is something wrong with my thyroid?" What I really wanted to say was, *What have you been looking at for the last five minutes?*

She seemed to be getting flustered as she went from pushing keys on the keyboard to staring at the monitor, flipping through my chart, and moving the wand left and right and around and around over my neck. Then she called to the other woman working at her desk. "Can you come over here?"

Something wasn't right. *Is there something wrong with the machine? Or is she new to this?* They kept their voices low, so I couldn't hear everything, but my technician seemed to be asking the other if the equipment was working properly. Then they started double-checking all the cords. I couldn't help but ask, "Is something wrong?"

They did not respond.

While they were occupied with the machine, I lifted my hand off the side of the examination table and moved it to my throat. Under my fingertips, I could still feel the lump. I wanted to believe it was gone, but of course, it wasn't, and I didn't want to have to come back for another ultrasound if this one didn't go right. Reluctantly, I spoke up.

"Excuse me, it's right here."

The technician opened my gown a bit more and applied more jelly to the wand, running it up and down my neck again in the place I had indicated. Hoping to get another look, I stretched to try to see the images, but she had turned the monitor away from my view. Then I heard a rapid *tap*, *tap*, *tap* on the keyboard accompanied by a clicking sound from the monitor. *Was that the sound of a successful ultrasound?*

I knew that technicians aren't allowed to diagnose or say anything about the images, but that didn't stop me from asking, "Do you see something?"

"Yes."

"What is it?"

Just as I expected, she simply stated, "I am not allowed to say."

Does she have to be so by the book? I knew she was only doing her job, but it was my throat, after all. But when she said, "Please wait here while I get the radiologist. I need him to take a look," I thought, *What is going on?*

Soon, the radiologist, wearing a very official-looking white coat, hurried in with his resident in tow. "Do you mind if I take a look?" he said and placed the wand directly on the bump. The whole appointment had been such an odd experience that I didn't mind them bringing in the doctor, but once he was in the room, his air of authority startled me. What did they see that made them call him in?

He looked at the monitor and asked, "Will you please sit up?" Next thing I know, he began doing the all-too-familiar finger dance across my neck and collarbone. Then he asked his resident to feel it as well. Without a word, I sat there, hoping it would end soon. I knew Mom would be terribly worried I had been in there so long, for a scan we'd been told would take five minutes. At least inside the exam room I knew what was going on. But Mom was in the waiting room, oblivious, and I knew this wouldn't sit well with her. I thought the doctor would be at liberty to tell me what he was seeing, so I asked again. "What is it?"

"I have to further review the images from your scan, then I will let your doctor know."

By then, I didn't know what to think. I just said, "Okay, thank you," as he left the room.

.... ❧ ....

Later that afternoon I dozed off watching TV and awoke to my sister, Carey, yelling out, "Hey, Susan, the phone's for you."

As I went downstairs to grab the phone, I mouthed, "Who is it?"

"Dr. Seyfried," she answered.

Immediately, I thought, *It's 5:45. It's after hours.* I quickly picked up. "Hello, this is Susan."

"Hi, Susan. This is Dr. Seyfried." Not waiting for a response, he continued, "I have the results from your testing. Are your parents home? Can you put one of them on the phone?"

My heart began to race. I dropped the phone and yelled down the hallway, "Mom. Mom! Pick up the phone. It's Dr. Seyfried." With the phone back at my ear, I heard Mom on the other end.

"Hi, Laura. The results are in. Susan, the ultrasound indicated there is nothing wrong with your thyroid." That was great. I'd been preparing to hear how we were going to fix my thyroid, and it turned out it was nothing. But Dr. Seyfried wasn't finished. He said slowly and clearly, "But we are dealing with an enlarged lymph node."

A lymph node?

I clenched the phone and stood there, frozen. *Oh no—Dad and Aunt Sue. They had lymph node problems, and it was cancer.* Quiet tears streamed down my face. It felt like the air had been sucked out of me. I quickly collected myself to ask, "What do we do now?"

Dr. Seyfried's voice went muffled, as if he were talking

to me underwater. It didn't matter. I knew Mom would listen carefully. He said something about needing more testing, meeting with a specialist, and possibly surgery. I hung up the phone with the words *lymph node* ringing in my ears.

I stood there stunned, confused, and overwhelmed. Mom must have sprinted down the hallway because by the time I walked out of the room, she was right there. With her arms around me in a steadfast grip, Mom whispered, "I am so sorry. So, so sorry."

I was too.

With slumped shoulders and my head down, I went to my room, still stunned. I'd been waiting for an answer, and the one we got only presented more questions. I was sitting on my bed when my parents came into the room. Mom looked the way I felt. Her face was crestfallen, and she wasn't saying a word. Not wanting to rehash the call, I asked, "What about school? I have a twenty-page paper due and a final presentation in Communications Strategy. I have to go back—"

"We knew that was going to be your main concern," Dad said, cutting me off. "Write down your teachers' names and email addresses, and I will contact them. You need to get in for a CAT scan as soon as possible."

As Dad was talking, I couldn't help but notice Mom's look of distress. Selfishly, I was happy Mom had been on the other end of the phone with me, but I was sorry too. I wished I could have spared her from hearing what Dr. Seyfried had to say. She seemed trapped in her own thoughts, although I'm pretty sure we were thinking the same thing: *Dad has lymph node problems, and it's cancer. Aunt Sue had lymph node problems, and she died.*

Two days later, I had a CAT scan. While I should have been out drinking margaritas and beer with my friends at school, I was sitting between Mom and Dad drinking contrast, this gloppy, gross white stuff, for the scan. The contrast was a kind of dye that would highlight the places the doctor needed to see.

The test didn't hurt, but the endless possibilities of what it might reveal were painful in a way I'd never known before. Dad's lymphoma had been known to show up throughout his body. I worried, *What if I'm like Dad? What if I have more than one spot?* I lay staring at the white hospital ceiling and, so I wouldn't let my heavy breathing get the best of me, began praying the Hail Mary over and over in my head. I had never really understood what my dad had gone through during his cancer treatment. I was concerned when Dad went for scans, of course, but I didn't really know what he went through up until that day, and I was upset with myself for never fully realizing how scary the process must have been for him. It was certainly terrifying for me.

We waited for the results. I went back and forth between school and home and the hospital for more tests, trying to keep things as routine as possible. I'd find myself sitting in class, absentmindedly running my fingers along the bump on my throat. The question *What is it?* was constantly lurking in the back of my mind. It was exhausting. Weeks went by, with tests every week and long weekends in between, and still no end in sight. Finally, Dr. Jackson, an ear, nose, and throat specialist, recommended surgery. I was relieved to have a plan to move forward, but as my mom worked with the doctor to schedule the procedure, I felt my life spiraling out of control.

No one asked me what I wanted or what I thought. I wanted to say, *What about me?* But I just kept showing up and politely following along without any protest. What else was there to do?

Once Dr. Jackson had decided surgery was the right course of action, I was supposed to have the procedure right away, but Mom bargained with him to let me go back to school for a week, which she knew was important to me. At home, things felt unsettled and out of place. At school, I could keep things normal and routine. I didn't tell anyone about my testing. I'm not totally sure why I kept it to myself, but I did. Maybe just because I could—it was one small way of staying in control.

Besides, canceling plans was not something I liked to do. I had a term paper to work on, a group presentation, upcoming finals, and a résumé to write—remember that black suit. The Relay For Life charity event I had signed up for in the fall also happened to be that weekend. I wasn't going to be known as Susan Carver Stachler, the Girl Who Quits. I had planned on being at this event all year, and right then, I needed something to go as I had planned. I welcomed this distraction and figured it would keep my mind off things. So, back to school I went.

Sponsored by the American Cancer Society, Relay For Life is a well-known, twenty-four-hour outdoor event that raises money for cancer research. I was in charge of the luminaria event, raising money by selling personalized paper bags with candles inside, which would be lined up around the track that participants would be walking during the relay and lit at nightfall as a glowing tribute to those affected by the disease. All I knew was that I'd better sell the bejeebers out of those bags, or else we were going to have one sorry, unlit track, and it would be all my fault. All spring I had been writing letters to faculty and staff, setting up a card table in the middle of campus to solicit donations, and providing donation forms to all the local pizza places around town, which taped them to the top of their delivery boxes.

I'd be lying if I didn't say that I was proud of myself as I walked onto the empty football field the day of the event to begin setting up. I was proud to be a part of something good. Did I think about the connection between Relay For Life and my testing? Not really. But maybe Mom did—she kept trying to get me to skip the event and stay home for the weekend.

Once the other committee members arrived, we began setting up the stage, sound system, welcome tent, concession stand, and all the other thousand details I had been working on for months.

My last task before the event started was to put the luminarias together. The final tally was in, and I had hundreds of names to write on white paper bags; my family and Randy arrived just in time to help. Mom and I wrote on the bags, Dad and Randy dropped sand and a candle into each one, and then volunteers placed them evenly about every ten inches around the perimeter of the track.

With the sun nearly down, the sky was filled with stars. Fireflies flickered in the trees, and a positive, lively energy arose from the students gathered on the field amid this stunning display of lights. In order to get a better view, I moved up high in the bleachers. For all the times I'd jogged around that track, I had never paid attention like I did standing there that evening. I appreciated being there in a different way. The scene played out in slow motion as I looked down to see my classmates laughing and smiling. I'd been keeping the details of my medical testing to myself, not even sharing them with my closest friends, and for a moment I longed for their innocence.

The stadium lights dimmed and the head of the event announced, "Please make your way to the track, as we're about to begin the luminaria ceremony." Students began quietly walking to the soft music floating from the speakers, and I made my way to the stage in the center of the field.

By then it was dark, apart from the glow from the flickering candles, and a single spotlight beamed down on me. Someone handed me a microphone and a clipboard. Along with selling and preparing the luminarias, it was my responsibility to read out the names of the people to whom they had been dedicated. My heart was thumping. I didn't usually get nervous in front of crowds, but as I held the list of names, reality sank in. The names on that paper were not merely names. They were grandfathers and grandmothers, moms and dads, brothers and sisters, aunts, uncles, and friends—the names of people who had mattered to my classmates—some of whom had survived cancer, and some of whom had not.

I began. "In memory of… In honor of…" The stadium fell silent as I read hundreds of names, focusing on one at a time, and then, before I had registered the words on the page in front of me, I read aloud, "In honor of Ken Stachler." I looked up to find Dad and was surprised to see my parents standing alone, off to the side of the stage, watching me. I smiled.

I put my head back down to find my place on the list, opening my mouth to keep reading—but nothing came out. *Come on, Susan, just read.* I couldn't. The next name on the list jumped off the page. It was my aunt's name…but my name too. I had known Aunt Sue would be on this list. Granny and Grandpa had sent me their donation form, and it certainly wasn't like I was just learning for the first time Aunt Sue had died from cancer. But my heart was racing, tears were pooling in my eyes, and I knew if I spoke I'd have a quiver in my voice. *Next year, is some college kid going to be up here reading my name?* For the first time since the nurse practitioner had discovered the lump on my throat, I was afraid. *Do I have cancer?*

Standing on the platform trying to do my part for a fundraiser was not the time to be thinking of myself, but I couldn't help it. *Just read the name.* I stood there fumbling for what was probably all of a few seconds, but it felt like an eternity. If I looked up, I knew Mom would rush to my side. If I had given her the slightest hint that I was in trouble, she would have run up there, taken me off that stage, put her arms around me, and made someone else finish reading. But I didn't want to crumble. I wanted to be strong. And then it was out, reverberating over the football field and into the night.

"In memory of Susan Carver Smith."

Dear Sue,

I sure didn't want Susan to go back to school during her testing. I was already feeling protective of her—it was hard to see her leave. I think I felt that if she stayed at home with me, everything would be okay. Nothing bad would happen. It was right, though, for her to go. You made doctors wait for you sometimes when you had other plans. Susan was so determined to go back, they would wait for her too. At least for a few days.

I have to tell you, it was extraordinary to see Susan stand on the platform at the Relay For Life event. It was a peaceful night. Ken and I stood in the distance. All I could see was Susan glowing under one spotlight. Then I heard her voice—slowly, distinctly, reading out the names. And, in my head, I heard my silent, pleading prayer, begging God, "Please let what I fear most pass over Susan." I heard Ken's name echo through the stadium. Then, Susan said your name.

3

Going, Going, Gone

MONDAY MORNING CAME QUICKLY, AND I FOUND myself sitting in the outpatient surgery lobby at Saint Joseph's Hospital with my parents and Randy. It was time for this thing at the base of my neck, which I refused to call a tumor, to go. As much as I hated waking up so early, I was ready to get this done.

Dad broke the uncomfortable silence. "What kind of polish do they use on these floors? I wonder what they use to get them so shiny. Hey, Randy, did you know I have a commercial floor buffer?"

I was grateful for the mindless chatter, especially when the conversation turned to food. As soon as Mom asked, "Anyone want a sandwich from East Forty-Eighth Street Market?" we began discussing what we would eat later. In between determining whether I'd have the club sandwich or roast beef and waiting for my name to be called, I jumped a little every time the double doors to our right swung open.

I felt edgy, even though I knew I had no need to worry. I was in good hands with Dr. Jackson. As soon I met him, I liked him—he was friendly, low-key, calm, talked in terms I understood, and still had a level of cockiness I appreciated. When he assured me, "I'll make a nice, clean incision. It'll be flawless," I believed him. Besides, he'd been Dad's doctor too, so I'd seen his work. With one slice on his neck, another on his shoulder, two to the chest, and one across the stomach, Dad vouched for Dr. Jackson's workmanship.

When a nurse finally came out to the waiting room and called, "Susan? Susan Stachler?" I leaped out of my seat. I thought I would be doing this alone, but I turned around to see Mom one step behind me.

"Okay if I come along?" she asked.

So the two of us walked briskly behind the nurse down the corridor. Finally, she stopped and pulled back a curtain blocking the entrance to a small cubicle, indicating we'd reached our station. Mom sat in the side chair, and I took a seat on the hospital bed. The nurse took my vitals while she carefully went over what was about to take place. I thought the nurse was making the surgery sound rather routine, but Mom was obviously not feeling that way—she had slid her rosary out from her purse and hidden it in her palm.

I wondered, *Are her prayers for me?* I hoped not. I felt fine. Maybe they were for the surgeon. Better yet, I hoped they were for herself. Between the two of us, I felt Mom was the one who could use some backup. She didn't say much, but I knew she was concerned.

Then the nurse asked me a strange question: "Where are you having surgery?" After I pointed to the center of my collarbone, she marked my skin with a black *X* and said, "This is to ensure that no mistakes are made and that we all understand what surgery is being performed and where." Apparently, this was standard procedure, but it made me laugh a little.

With this new "*X* marks the spot" on my skin, I couldn't help but smile, thinking about the night before. The seven of us—my family plus Randy—had gathered around the kitchen table for a delicious meal Mom made for me. Home-cooked food is how Mom shows love. She made this dinner as her way of saying, *We are a family, we care about each other, and tomorrow it's all about Susan.*

Near the end of the meal, Dad addressed the elephant in the room. "By tomorrow night, Susan will have a permanent smiley face across her neck."

"Ken!" called Mom from the counter where she was dishing up dessert.

"Dad! A little sympathy?" I said. I gestured to my neck. "You better take a good look at my beautiful neck now. Last chance!"

My brothers, catching on that it was acceptable to crack a few jokes, joined in, and while Mom attempted to shut them up, that only provoked them to keep going. We're not a mushy, sensitive group, so I reveled in the teasing.

Now, in less than an hour, I'd have a permanent line along my neck. In the grand scheme of things, I knew this scar was nothing to complain about, but I can't say I was pumped about it.

With my long blond hair tucked into a surgical hairnet and a hospital gown tied around me, I was enveloped from head to toe in a lovely shade of medical blue. Dressed and ready, I climbed into the bed and pulled the blankets over me. Mom still looked unsettled, and I think she would have liked to hop on the gurney and lie down next to me if she could have.

"Mom, the best news of the day?" I said to break the uneasy silence. "I get to keep my underwear on."

With a laugh she said, "That's what you're thinking about?"

"Yes! Mom, you have to agree. Don't you think it's weird for the doctors to make you take your underwear off? Especially if the surgery is on your neck. I was talking with Steph about this last night."

Mom was cracking up, so I recounted the conversation with my best friend. "Steph told me she asked her doctor once why you have to take everything off when you have surgery, and he said it's in case something goes wrong, they won't have to cut your clothes off. Can you believe it?"

Mom was still laughing.

"Let me just tell you," I added. "If something goes so wrong that they have to cut my clothes off, I think I'll have a lot more to worry about than a ruined outfit!"

Our laughter ended as another nurse entered and started hooking me up to a few machines and prepping my arm for the IV. Mom slipped out to get Dad and brought him back to wait with me. Soon enough, the meds were dripping into my veins. The nurse unlocked the brakes on the bed, popped the side rails up, and said to my parents, "Give your daughter a kiss. We'll take good care of her."

I started to feel loopy. Mom leaned in, kissed the top of my head, then casually slid a saint's relic into my sock. She'd waited until the drugs had kicked in because she knew I would protest. But I figured, *If it's going to make her feel better, then why not?* Seeing Mom's eyes gloss over with tears, I assured my parents, "I'll see you soon. Tell Randy I'll be right out."

My parents disappeared, and the nurse's face loomed over me. "Susan, count backward from ten."

I woke up crying—my usual reaction to general anesthetic. It had happened with my wisdom teeth and my tonsils, so I knew it would happen after this surgery too. The nurse hovering over me said, "Susan, you're out of surgery. It went well."

But my uncontrollable tears kept coming, even as he begged,

"You have to stop crying. You're going to upset your family. They're already worried, since your surgery took longer than expected."

I had no idea what he was talking about.

As he wheeled me back to my original room, he asked, "Do you think you can give a big wave when you see your parents?"

Mom, Dad, and Randy were already waiting for me. Mom filled the air. "Honey, you're all done! You did great." I thought that was a funny thing to say, considering all I had to do was lie on a table. But it was reassuring to hear her continue, "We just saw Dr. Jackson, and he is very pleased with his work. He said it looks great, and he kept the incision as small as he could."

I wasn't sure how fantastic it could look, because it felt like an entire roll of toilet paper had been taped around the middle of my collarbone to cover up a huge gash. It was great the surgery was over and everyone was happy about how I apparently did well and how the doctor left an amazingly perfect mark on me, but I wanted to know what he thought about the lump. "Mom, what is it? What did Dr. Jackson say?"

"He won't know for a few days. He'll call us once the results are in. But you did great. Really, really great. Dad and I are so proud of you."

.... 🌿 ....

Finding out that it could take up to ten days to get the results back was devastating—it might as well have been a year. The doctor had taken the lump out, and now the tissue had to cultivate in some lab before it could be diagnosed. *How gross!*

Even though people kept telling me there was a problem with my lymph nodes, no one, I mean *no one*—not even the doctors—ever mentioned the possibility of cancer or anything to do with lymphoma. It was odd no one came right out and said they were testing for cancer, but under the circumstances, with Dad still going through chemo and Aunt Sue's history, everyone was being extra sensitive.

Two days later, I was still sore, but I insisted I was good to go back to school. My professors had agreed I could end the year with the grades I'd already earned, but I was determined to finish out the year. One afternoon after class, I left the business building, plodding along with only the necessary books under my arm. I had tried putting on my backpack, but it felt like my incision was going to rip wide open. I probably looked weird, slouched over and hobbling along, but I didn't care. I liked being on campus, even if I was exhausted and felt strangely removed from my surroundings, as if I were stuck in my own little world of worry. It just didn't make sense. *Why is any of this happening? The timing is stupid. This whole thing is kind of stupid.* And then I wondered, *Did I do something wrong?*

I was uneasy, waiting for the phone call that could come in at any minute. The plan was for the doctor to call Mom, and then she would call me. Since I was over eighteen, I had to sign a waiver allowing the doctors to talk to my parents about my medical issues.

It was a no-brainer. I figured, *If there's something wrong, call Mom. That's what she's there for.*

Arriving back at my apartment, I was hoping to open the door and see a message from my mom waiting for me. But there was nothing. So I called her.

As soon as she said hello, I dove right in. "Hi, Mom, have you heard anything?"

"Not yet," she said calmly. "I promise, I will call you when I know something."

"Why don't they know yet?"

"Honey, please try not to think about it until we hear something."

Frustrated and slightly troubled, I kept pushing. "What are they looking for? What do you think it is? If you were to guess, what would you guess it is?"

"I can't guess because we haven't heard anything," said Mom.

"Has Dad said anything? What does Dad think it is? Maybe they forgot to call us."

"Sweetie, they didn't forget you. How are your classes? Did you come up with a topic for your research paper?"

"Mom, maybe you should call and see."

She sighed. "Let's give it another day."

I tried one more time, even though I knew I would just have to wait. "So, Dr. Jackson has no clue? No idea? He seriously doesn't know?"

I knew I was pestering, but I couldn't help it. I wanted her to say out loud what I had started to think, but she was barely saying anything. Her calmness was driving me bananas.

After hanging up, I felt guilty, so I called back. "Hi, Mom. It's me. I'm sorry I'm bothering you."

"It's fine. You call as much as you want."

"I'm sorry about all of this. And I hung up before I even asked you how things are going with the shop."

Earlier in the year, Mom had decided to move ahead with turning our garage into a bakery, naming her new business Laura's Divine Desserts. Maybe I should have thought it was a crazy idea, but I didn't. I was excited for her. Our garage was a detached building with a basement. Mom explained the kitchen would be on the main level, where she would bake and people could pick up orders, and the office would be set up below.

For the next forty-five minutes, Mom and I were back to having one of our usual phone calls, discussing cheesecake flavors, the details of her recent big order from our orthodontist, and how she had already burned out her mixer.

Toward the end of the week, Mom apparently got very "busy," since she had Dad calling me every day before I could call home. And Dad, well, he didn't leave much room for asking questions.

My emotions had been brewing for weeks, and they finally boiled over one night while I was trying to study. I sat cross-legged on my bed, staring down at my open three-ring binder. I needed to learn the information and I couldn't. I tried to keep my focus on the notes and test-prep papers laid out in front of me, but I could not concentrate. Tears pooled in my eyes, and the words on the page turned blurry. I was consumed by my thoughts, fears, and worries, which had gone wild. *I can't take this*, I thought. Randy was sitting in the other room, and I could hear the rumble of the TV. In a frenzy, I burst out of my room, crying out, "I did this to myself. I did this!"

Randy turned the TV down, looking stunned. "What?"

"I think I willed this to happen to me," I said, almost yelling. "I think I willed myself to get cancer." Randy's look went from puzzled to alarmed. Through my tears, I explained, "I always wanted to know what it was like to be my aunt Sue. I wanted to know how she felt, what it was like to live with her disease. And now it's happening to me."

Randy didn't say anything. By then I was trembling. "If this is cancer, if I have cancer, it will not stop me. I'm not changing. I'm not going to sit around and be sick."

It all came out in a rush. Poor Randy. I felt awful, but I needed someone to hear me. I needed to say it out loud. Thankfully, Randy didn't try to stop me. He just listened.

We stared at each other. Everything stopped. Randy reached for his wallet. "I'll be right back." I watched him walk out the door, upset and confused.

Twenty minutes later, Randy was back with more food than

we could possibly eat, covering the entire surface of the coffee table with to-go containers that he pulled out of a paper bag. "I didn't know what to get you. I got cheese dip, chips, guacamole, tacos, and a burrito. I thought maybe you'd like the quesadilla? Suz, have whatever you want."

We sat on the couch, enjoyed our Mexican food, and turned on a movie. Sitting there with him, surrounded by the food he had brought as a thoughtful gesture to comfort me, I felt just a little bit better.

Dear Sue,

We had gone through a string of tests and found nothing conclusive. But I knew where it was leading. And I was becoming afraid that Susan might know too. I was trying so hard to be casual and brush off her questions, but I think she saw right through me. Even Ken and I never discussed the possibility of Susan having cancer.

After her surgery was over, we had to wait days for the results. I called at the first opportunity the doctor had given us to check in and was told to call back the next day. I got the same response the next time I called. I was turning into a wreck. The third time I called, as soon as the nurse started to say that she didn't think there was any news, I pleaded with her to double-check. "My husband and I have been waiting for days. Could you please see if the lab results are in for Susan Stachler?" I held on the line, switching the phone from my left hand to my right while wiping the sweat that was beading up on my palms onto my jeans. Finally, I heard someone come back on the line. "This is Dr. Jackson."

4

So That's What It Feels Like

A WEEK HAD PASSED. IT WAS TIME TO GO HOME TO get my stitches out, and I was looking forward to it. I wanted to hear what Dr. Jackson had to say.

Arriving home, I noticed that something was off as soon as I opened the back door. The house was silent and dark, and in a family of six, that never happened. I made my usual trek through the house, down the back hallway to my bedroom. As I passed the kitchen, I saw Mom rummaging through the refrigerator. She seemed really focused on finding some long-lost jar of pickles or something, and she didn't look up or say hello to me, which wasn't like her at all. I reached my bedroom, dropped my bags, and put some ChapStick on. In the midst of my usual five-minute routine, it dawned on me. *I bet she knows.*

Coming around the corner with a cheerful "Hi, Mom!" I

took a seat at the counter. Mom was on one side of the kitchen island; I was on the other.

Fidgeting and twirling two empty glasses around and around, Mom asked, "Would you like a drink? I just made lemonade."

"Sure. Thanks," I said.

Mom looked drained. Her eyes were tired and her brow was furrowed. I didn't like seeing her like this. Once the glasses were filled, she began tapping her fingernails on the countertop. "I'll pour Dad some too." Dad walked in and took a seat near me.

Mom turned her back to us, and as she put the pitcher in the refrigerator door, she took a deep breath. "So… We got the results. We'd been waiting to hear from Dr. Weens."

Dr. Weens? I thought. *That's Dad's doctor. She's an oncologist. I didn't know she was part of this.*

Mom turned around and faced me. "You have a treatable form of cancer. *Treatable.* Sweetie, you have Hodgkin's disease."

I sat there and stared at Mom's face, relief washing over me. I felt like I had been holding my breath for weeks, and now I could finally inhale. But, then… *Wait, what? Hodgkin's? I have Hodgkin's.* I thought I had heard Mom clearly, but I had to ask. "It's Hodgkin's?"

"I'm so sorry."

Mom repeated her well-rehearsed mantra. "It's treatable, curable, things are different now." I knew Mom didn't want me to think about Aunt Sue, but it was too late.

Dad moved over and sat right next to me, and Mom came around the counter to join us. My head went down, and I stared at my hands folded tightly in my lap. *So this is what it feels like? I have cancer. It's what I expected, but it feels different.* And just as I was settling into one thought, another one came up. *But, Hodgkin's—how can this be? Of all things? Oh, Mom... Aunt Sue. She died from this...* Tears streamed down my face.

My parents didn't move. I wasn't angry or scared, but in that moment, everything just seemed unreal. I clearly remember thinking, *I can do this.* My parents were waiting for my reaction. I needed to let them know I was okay. It was then that I realized I had a choice—it was my choice how to handle things.

I let out a chuckle. "It's my name. It's all because you named me Susan. You should have called me Frank, then this never would have happened!"

"Susan!"

I swear, they were almost exuberant with my response. They'd been holding their breath too. Dad laughed a little and seemed relieved I wasn't a total mess, but it was a fleeting moment. Seeing Mom in such pain, my heart broke and my tears started up again.

"Mom, how long have you known?"

"We had an idea after your surgery."

They've been holding this news in all this time? I asked, "What do you mean you've had an idea?"

"Dr. Jackson talked to us in the lobby after your surgery. He said the tumor was larger than he expected, which is why the surgery took longer. Honey, the part you could feel was just the top of the tumor. He said it was the size of his fist, and it went down toward your heart." She paused, then added, "That's why Dr. Jackson was pleased with the incision. He worked to keep it as small as possible."

"What else did he say?" I asked.

Mom patiently answered each of my questions. I could tell she was concerned that I'd be mad at her for keeping this information from me. I wasn't, but I did want to know every detail. She continued, "He came out and said, 'It looks like cancer.'"

Oh my gosh. Mom and Dad. That must have been terrible.

Becoming distressed, I asked, "In the lobby? Mom, does Randy know?"

She nodded her head slowly. "He was sitting right next to me. I wish he hadn't been."

I could not stop crying. "Randy knew? He never said anything." My heart sank. *Randy heard that I have cancer.* It was starting to make sense why Randy had seemed distant for the last week, why the only thing he could do when I broke down was to comfort me with Mexican food. He didn't know what to say. He was around, but he wasn't acting like himself. Then I cried even more, remembering how I had uncharacteristically yelled at him. *Do you have any idea what it's like to worry about someone? What's wrong with you?* He walked out the door and didn't come back for hours. I had no idea what was going on.

"Don't be mad at him," Mom said.

"I'm not. I just…" My mind was racing.

"He followed our wishes," she explained. "If you want to be mad, be mad at me. I told him not to tell you. I was very sorry that he'd heard what Dr. Jackson said, but I had to ask him not to say anything to you until we knew for sure."

Mom paused for a moment, but I could see in her face she had something else to say.

"Who else knows?" My voice rose. "Do Granny and Grandpa know?"

"Yes."

"No!" I exclaimed. "No, you didn't tell them." I was sobbing now. It was bad enough envisioning Mom and Dad and Randy hearing this news, but Granny and Grandpa? The image of them sitting in their recliners in their den, getting the news over speakerphone that I had the same disease their daughter had died from was more than I could bear. My grandparents were tough and lovely, but they were also getting old.

The more I learned about who knew about my diagnosis, the more dreadful it was. I felt an indescribable sadness. I didn't want anyone worrying about me.

"What about the kids? Did you tell them?" I asked. I

couldn't imagine what it would be like for my brothers and sister to hear about my cancer.

Mom seemed drained too. "I told Luke right before you got home, and I've called Robert. Dad is planning to tell Carey when he picks her up from school today."

"Carey? No. Do we have to tell her?" Through my tears, I managed to get out, "Mom, you could have told me, you know."

Mom looked over to Dad, and he chimed in. "Dr. Weens told us not to."

Mom explained that Dr. Weens would not make a diagnosis until she had reviewed all the tests herself and the final results were in. She'd been concerned about the possibility of non-Hodgkin's lymphoma, a worse form of the disease, and wanted to rule that out first. *Oh, dear God*, I thought. *So Mom was praying all week that I would be diagnosed with the disease that killed her sister, rather than the one that Dad has?*

"What happens now?"

Mom's eyes locked on mine. "I'll tell you what we're going to do," she said. "For now, you're going to go back to school, finish your classes, be with your friends. You're going to have fun and you're going to graduate and we're all going to be there to see you, as planned. Dr. Weens said to enjoy graduation, and she'll see you in two weeks."

As I prepared to go back to school on Monday, I wasn't scared about my diagnosis—I was relieved. Finally, the lump had a name, and we could put together a plan to treat it. I was worried about Mom though. I couldn't imagine what this must be like for her. Most of all, I was afraid that when she looked at me now, all she would see was her sister.

Dear Sue,

I had to call Mother and Dad and tell them that Susan had been diagnosed with your cancer. They were waiting to hear from me, so when I heard Mother's voice, I simply said, "It's Hodgkin's."

There was no response.

"Mother? Are you there?"

Her voice was barely audible. "Dad's out, and I'm sitting here alone, crying."

You know Mother never cried. Ever.

I said to her, "I don't think I can do this again."

She replied, "All right, honey. Yes you can."

Honestly, hearing those words didn't help. "You don't understand," I said, more firmly. "I'm telling you, I can't do this again." I started to unravel. "God help me, I can't watch her go through this. Why does this keep happening to me?" The minute I'd said that, I detested hearing my own selfishness, but I continued, screaming now. "I know everyone in the family loved Sue, but just tell me once, please, that you know Sue was also my best friend. I only wanted to name Susan for my sister, and now she has the same disease." I wailed, "What am I going to do?"

"Laura. Laura," Mother said reassuringly. "You're going to be strong. You've done this before."

"I don't want to do it again," I said. "I can't."

I had held this in for weeks. I'd kept it from Ken, our kids, my friends. And I'd kept it from Susan. I screamed at Mother like I'd never done in my life. "I can't watch Susan get sick. She's going to get sick."

Sue, because of you, I feared the worst.

5

Aunt Sue,
Meg Ryan,
and *Pretty Woman*

GRADUATION DAY ARRIVED, THE CULMINATION OF MY
four years at college, and I couldn't believe that it had finally
come. As I sat there in my cap and gown, I tried taking in the
moment, but it wasn't exactly what I'd envisioned. I was happy I
had a yellow cord around my neck signifying my induction into
the honor society, an asterisk next to my name in the program for
maintaining a high GPA, and my family in the stands, including
Granny and Grandpa, who'd flown in from San Diego. And yet,
it wasn't quite right.

From my seat in a plastic chair on the basketball court,
I heard the commencement speaker's words—"endless possibilities…exciting futures…the world's your oyster"—but they

didn't seem to apply to me. As I looked around at the sea of my fellow classmates dressed in shiny, navy blue robes and funny cardboard caps, I realized no one else in that vast arena was in my predicament. I would step onto the stage a college student and walk off a cancer patient. My diploma was my ticket to Dr. Weens's office. I couldn't sort out or control what was happening to me, and I didn't know what my future would hold. All I knew was I wouldn't be wearing that black interview suit anytime soon.

When I went up to receive my diploma, I stopped at the edge of the stage to look up to my family. They were clapping, hooting, and hollering for me. Dad was beaming, but my brothers and Randy looked slightly bored. I couldn't look at Mom. Right then, I was still Susan the student, and I played that role well. I put pressure on myself to perform and deflected any thoughts of cancer. I put up a front and just sort of floated through the day, working to be the best version of happy that I could be. I owed it to my family, but it took so much energy to keep up the facade that by the time our celebration lunch was over, I was worn out.

The following Monday, Mom, Dad, and I sat in a tiny exam room waiting for Dr. Weens. She had been Dad's doctor for more than a decade, but I'd never met her before. While I sat on the end of the examination table, Mom and Dad sat side by side directly in front of me. I wasn't nervous or worried. If anything, it was funny seeing my parents squished into two little chairs wedged between the door and the doctor's cabinet. The nurse had kindly brought in an extra chair, but there wasn't much space. We didn't wait long before Dr. Weens, a tiny, rather plain woman, came into the room.

She didn't mince words. I was instantly swamped with information and medical terms, and soon my brain became exhausted from trying to follow the conversation. I was feeling lost, until she uttered the words, "After further reviewing your results, we are looking at a combination of radiation and chemotherapy."

Chemotherapy. What? I had been under the impression I'd just need some radiation. I sat there not saying much at all, trying not to cry. I wanted to make a good impression on Dr. Weens. If I was brave, if I was strong, then I was in control. Besides, I didn't think I deserved the luxury of crying. At least I had my parents with me. I was not alone, and that was more comfort than I could possibly say. If I started crying now, the cancer would already be winning.

I braced myself by putting my hands on both sides of the examination table and leaned forward to try to hold up my end of the conversation. But all I was saying was a lot of, "Yes, okay, I can do that." I felt like I was sinking into myself. Nothing could have prepared me to hear the words, "You'll need chemo."

As Dr. Weens continued explaining the disease, the drugs, the advances in medicine and technology, I tuned out, stuck on the idea of chemotherapy. *I'm going to get sick. This will be miserable.*

And my hair. Will it fall out? What will I look like? And what about our trip to California?

My family was planning to go to San Diego the next week to see my younger brother, Luke, run a marathon for the Leukemia & Lymphoma Society. Months ago, I had suggested to Luke that he should run in it and raise money for cancer research. Now, along with Dad's and Aunt Sue's names, he would be adding my name to his jersey. We had also planned a few extra days to go to the San Diego Zoo, visit family and friends, and spend a day at the beach. Mom was probably going to take us to the cemetery to visit Aunt Sue's grave, then stop at her favorite Mexican restaurant to toast her afterward.

Even though I was wondering about whether my hair would fall out and if I could still go to California, I wasn't about to ask those questions now, partly because I didn't want to hear the answers, but also because we were dealing with a deadly disease. Dr. Weens's main concern was my life—not my hair or a family trip. So I sat there in silence, nodding my head every now and again.

For weeks, we'd been talking about my lump, then my cancer diagnosis, but treatment had always seemed far away. It never seemed real. But now, Mom and Dad were taking notes on all the appointments and tests I needed to have done: echocardiograms, biopsies, PET scans, meetings with my radiologist, facility tours, and surgery to implant a port for my chemotherapy. It was a lot to take in, and this would all be done over the next week!

I couldn't believe that any of this was happening, and at such a rapid speed.

Later that day, I asked Mom to call and leave a voicemail for the doctor, asking the questions I couldn't stop thinking about. Going on the California trip would mean pushing the start of chemo back one week. I crossed my fingers and hoped for the best.

.... ❧ ....

The next day, I sat at the kitchen counter, peacefully enjoying a snack. It was a quiet afternoon, and my parents were both working in the home office. Mom was tweaking the menu for her dessert business, and Dad, I imagine, was perfecting intricate financial spreadsheets for it. I could hear Mom walking through the dining room, the hardwood floors creaking under her feet. She stopped in the entrance of the kitchen. Her cheeks were pale and her expression deflated. I knew she'd reached Dr. Weens. I stayed seated on the kitchen stool, and Mom stayed planted in the doorway.

"Dr. Weens said she waited for you to graduate and has put off treatment as long as she can. You need to start chemo right away."

I understood what she'd said, but I still asked, "What does that mean?"

Mom answered, "We can't go to California. Dad's already called Delta. You and I can use the tickets another time."

"It can't wait until we get back? We seriously have to start chemo right now?" I didn't want to believe that this was so serious that four or five days would make a difference.

"That's what Dr. Weens said."

I felt frustrated and trapped, but I knew there was no sense in questioning the doctor's orders. I wasn't upset about not getting to see palm trees or feel the California sunshine. No, I was mad that cancer was making me cancel my plans. This was bad, and it was only going to get worse.

"Fine," I said, my frustration coming through in my voice. "Okay. What day then? When do I start?"

"She scheduled you for next Friday."

"Friday? June fourth?"

"Yes."

Is this a coincidence or some kind of bizarre joke? June fourth? I was starting my treatment on the anniversary of Aunt Sue's death. This couldn't get any eerier.

"Well, what about my hair? Will it fall out?"

Mom, who hadn't moved from the doorway, answered, "Honey, it's different for everyone. No two people are the same. But it can happen."

"Mom, what about me? What is going to happen to *me*?"

Mom nodded. She couldn't say it, so I did.

"It's going to fall out. My hair is going to fall out. Isn't it?"

Gently, she confirmed, "It probably will."

In that moment, my world was crushed. It was too much.

I grabbed a big handful of my long blond hair, pulling on it as I got up from the counter and crossed to the windows. The rush of emotions was physically painful. I stood there, shaking my head from side to side, but the realization that this disease was in control was more than I could shake off. For days, I'd tried with all my might to hold it together, but I couldn't do it this time.

The cancer was real, it was happening to me, and for a minute, I was furious. I held on to my hair and thought, *I can't escape treatment, and now I won't even be able to hide it. I wanted this to be private. Now it won't be.* I kept my back to Mom and the kitchen. *My life will never be the same.* Then, from somewhere deep inside me, I let out a bloodcurdling scream. It was a noise I'd never heard before. One that scared me.

Suddenly, Mom was grabbing onto me. "I'm right here," she said. Her voice broke.

And I lost it in a way that I never knew possible. I clung to my mom, sobbing, "No, no, please. I will never be the same. Mom, help me." I buried my head into her shoulder, my knees weak, my hands clenched as I wailed and repeatedly pounded my fist into her back. *I'll look like a cancer patient. I don't want to be different. I don't want this.* Mom didn't try to stop me. Instead, she allowed me to let it out. As my emotions took over, I collapsed onto her. *I have cancer.* It was one thing to hear that I had it, and another thing to really know it.

By the time Mom got me to the couch in the family room,

I was not only worn out, but also appalled with myself for having scared her like that. I had no idea all those feelings and fears were even in me. With my anguish on full display, we sat side by side. Mom placed her hand on my leg. "You're not doing this alone, Susan. I am right here."

.... ❧ ....

A few days later, we met with Dr. Weens's assistant, Carole, for our tour and meeting to go over my treatment and what to expect in the upcoming months. I'd visited Dad at the cancer center before, so the tour wasn't anything too new, although I was taking everything in from a new perspective. This time, I was the patient.

After being handed a new-patient welcome packet, I quickly flipped through the papers on all kinds of things, ranging from details about Hodgkin's to free yoga classes. There was also an information sheet on each drug I would take and the possible corresponding side effects. Carole methodically reviewed each one. "Be aware that this might cause loss of appetite, itchy skin, numbness of fingers, diarrhea, vomiting, bone pain, constipation, rash, swelling, fatigue, memory loss." And, for each drug we went over, she always ended with, "And this can cause hair loss."

Sensing that I was getting discouraged, Carole added, "Susan, you won't have all the side effects, but you might have some of them. Some people have more than others. You might have fewer." Bottom line: it's a calculated guess. Even the best doctors can't know how someone will react to any medication until they try it out.

I continued to flip through the packet and landed on a yellow flyer advertising a ten percent discount at Bernadettes Hair Salon and Wig Studio. Carole noticed and said, "You might want to consider having a wig ready by your first treatment."

There wasn't much I could do about the potential itchy skin, mouth sores, or numbing of my fingertips. So many variables were being thrown at me, and I don't like the unpredictable. So I grabbed onto the one thing I could do. I was going to get a wig.

As soon as we left, I handed Mom the flyer. "Will you call and see what this is all about?"

"Of course I will," she said. We did not discuss my hair falling out, nor did Mom make a big deal out of it. She knew it was painful for me to think about, but she also knew I wanted to get this wig thing "right," and she wasn't going to let me do it alone.

Over the next few days, I launched us on a wild-goose chase, searching for the perfect wig. Our first stop was Bernadettes, the local salon from the flyer. Since Mom had explained when she made the appointment that I was twenty-two years old with long, straight blond hair, the wig specialist already had a few wigs in hand. She pulled flesh-colored panty hose over my head to squash my hair down, and as she stuffed my hair into this cap, she said pointedly, "You won't have all this bulk when you wear your wig."

Before we had entered the shop, I had told myself to pretend wig shopping was like trying on different shoes, but it didn't feel like that. This wasn't fun.

I stared into the mirror, frozen and apprehensive, as the woman stretched a wig over my head. I saw myself reflected with brown hair flipped up and straight bangs. I looked like Aunt Sue's high school picture from 1966. The woman said, "Brown hair tends to look more natural, and having some bangs gives it a softer look too."

I didn't know if I wanted to cry, throw up, or laugh. I could see Mom's face—she too was aching. I wished I could put my head in my hands and disappear. I ended the visit quickly, saying, "I'll have to think about it."

After that appointment, I made a decision. I liked my hair, but if I couldn't keep it, I wanted someone else to enjoy it. It wasn't going to do anybody any good once it had fallen out. Mom made the arrangements, and we went to our salon to have them cut my hair so I could donate it. I can't say I wasn't hesitant, but I felt like I did the right thing. I left with a cute, chin-length bob and my eight-inch ponytail in a ziplock bag, ready to be donated for a wig for a woman battling cancer.

A few days later, we drove an hour to a wig warehouse. The place was outrageous! From floor to ceiling, the walls were lined with hairpieces, wigs, ponytails, and hair extensions as far as the eye could see. If I was going to find a wig, it would be here.

The woman assisting us was rattling off advice. "Dark roots look most natural" and "Short hair is fun and sassy." Then she said, "I have just the thing for you."

The woman plopped a short, curly wig with brown roots and white, frosted tips onto my head. I burst out laughing. The stylist kept fluffing the wig with a pick, and I felt bad for laughing so hard, but I couldn't help it. I looked exactly like Meg Ryan in *Top Gun*. The style was cute then, on her, in the mid-1980s. The timing of my uncontrollable giggling might not have been impeccable, but it felt good to laugh. Mom was waiting for my cue. Twisting around in the chair, I shrugged my shoulders. "It's all right," I said, pointing to my head. "It's funny!"

Finally, Mom said, "She can't decide today. We're going to pass."

Trying a new approach, I went online and found a man in downtown Atlanta who made customized human-hair wigs. Again, Mom said, "I'll make the call."

When we pulled up to an industrial park lined with brown cement buildings with no windows, I asked, "Mom, are you sure we're in the right place?"

"This is the correct address," she said, double-checking the paper where she had written it down.

With hardly any cars in the parking lot and no one around,

the place seemed creepy. "Do you think we should go in?" I started to laugh. "Mom, we should just leave." *What have I gotten us into?*

"I called to confirm this morning. He said he'd be here." Mom was determined to see this through for me. We got out of the car and knocked on the thick metal door. After a minute, the door opened and a quirky little man greeted us. He seemed pleasant enough, but I wasn't so sure about venturing into the dark, dungeon-like room behind him.

As we stepped inside, he slid the metal door closed behind us and switched the deadbolt, saying, "I like to keep the door locked. It can be a bad area."

It soon became evident that he both worked and lived here. The room was an open-concept loft space, which could be kind of cool. But my eyes were fixated on the barbershop chair bolted to the floor in the middle of the kitchen. There were no windows and no lights on, except for one that beamed down on this barber chair. After examining my hair and running his fingers through it, he invited us to sit at his desk and proceeded to open binders filled with swatches of human hair. But where were the wigs?

"What kind of hair are you interested in?"

What? I thought. *I don't know. Hair! Blond hair. Something that looks like mine. I just want to try on a wig. Actually, never mind, I don't need a wig. I want to know how we're getting out of here.*

I had no idea what to say. Luckily, Mom leaned forward and said, "We're looking for a little something that would be close to my daughter's hair right now. Can we try something on?"

Mom was doing her best, but every time the man glanced away, I poked her leg and whispered, "Let's get out of here." We were in the wrong place—this guy made stunning wigs for things like theatrical productions and parades. I don't think young women with cancer were his specialty. These wigs started at $3,000, and they took months to make. Not to mention the fact that he wanted to shave my head right then and there on the spot.

We didn't want to be rude after taking his time, so on our way out, Mom said, "You've given us a lot to consider. We'll call back."

After days of searching the internet from the comfort of our home office, a box from Revlon arrived in the mail. I opened the lid to find the platinum-blond bob I'd ordered inside. It was my color, the hair was straight, and I had opted for bangs, as recommended, but this little number looked like Julia Roberts's hooker wig in *Pretty Woman*. It was sassy and snazzy all right, and I felt downright ridiculous in it. But I had a wig. I propped it up on a tall drinking glass on my dresser. Assignment completed.

Looking back, I had known before we ever started the wig hunt that we would never find just the right one. The one I wanted wasn't one at all. I wanted a say. And I wanted the power to say, "No, no thank you" to each wig at each place. It turned out that what I needed was a plan. I couldn't control my hair falling out, but I could control how I wanted to be seen. It would be bandannas and scarves covering my head as my hair fell out. I made a choice that was best for me.

Dear Sue,

Chemo and hair loss. I hated it for you, and twenty-seven years later, I hated it for Susan. But I tried not to let her do it alone. During your last hospital stay, the doctors gave you a multidrug cocktail—it was all they could do. Weeks later, the last time we ever spoke, do you remember what you told me? "Laur, I'm going to have to get a wig," you said matter-of-factly.

With your thick, gorgeous, honey-brown hair, I didn't want this to be the truth. So I tried to convince you otherwise. "You've got so much hair, I bet you're not going to need one."

When you insisted, "It's falling out," I told you I'd be there. I was crushed for you, sorrier than I could say. It meant that you were sick all over again. We never went shopping, because you didn't live long enough to need a wig. Days later, when you were hospitalized, a nurse braided what was left of your hair so you'd look pretty when we said goodbye.

6

Two Susans,
One Day

IT WAS HAPPENING, WHETHER I LIKED IT OR NOT. THE
first day of chemo arrived, and I didn't need my alarm to wake up
on time. I had never fully fallen asleep, tossing and turning in bed
for hours.

What will it feel like? How sick will I get? How bad is it going to be?

When I heard Mom in the kitchen that morning, I called
down the hall, "I'll be ready to go soon."

She'd already had an early morning, dropping Dad, Luke,
and Carey off at the airport. Since I could no longer go on the
trip to California, Mom got stuck staying here with me. She
didn't see it this way, but I did.

"Take your time," Mom responded. "I'm going to make
Italian sandwiches and pack the cooler with drinks and snacks."

She didn't say it, but I knew she was referring to our

chemo cooler. How could I have forgotten? I might have thought it bizarre that she'd kept that thing, were it not for the fact that Dad still had to have follow-up chemo periodically. The cooler held two sandwiches and eight drinks perfectly, and she'd been using it for years to keep Dad comfortable at his chemo treatments. It was stashed in our attic alongside the beach umbrella and camping chairs, like it was totally normal. I smiled, feeling pretty sure our family was the only one with a designated chemo cooler—you've got to love our sense of humor. Mom was packing up as if we were going on a picnic, but we were headed off to a day of treatment, where I'd be hooked up to an IV that would administer various drugs for nearly eight hours. I was repeatedly told that chemo days would be long and that I might not feel well, so I pulled on comfy clothes. *If I don't look sick, I won't be sick. If I look well, I will be well.* That became my mantra as I got ready, carefully doing my hair and makeup.

From the kitchen, I heard Mom say, "Hon, you ready? Meet you at the car."

On the silent ride to the hospital, I worried about Mom. On June 4, 1977, she left the hospital without her sister. Now, on June 4, 2004, she was heading to the hospital with her eldest daughter for treatment for the same disease. I thought about my little sister. Carey and I are six years apart. She's the person I call, talk to, hang out with, laugh with. I cannot imagine how

I would feel if anything happened to Carey. When I think about Mom carrying on without her sister, it's tragic. The bond between sisters who also happen to become best friends is unmatchable. That bond between Mom and Aunt Sue ended because of some disease, and that's hard to understand.

As I looked over at Mom, I thought, *If she can be strong, I can too. I want to show Mom it won't be that bad this time.*

After we pulled into the hospital parking lot, Mom jumped out of the car, ready to go. She had her purse, a tote filled with snacks and magazines, and our special cooler hooked over one arm, and a fuzzy, leopard-print fleece blanket rolled up and stuffed under the other.

"Mom, can I take something?" I offered.

"No," she responded, abruptly. "I've got it. This I can do."

I let her be and followed one step behind as she marched toward the sliding glass doors. Mom had told me, "If I could do this for you, I would." What she didn't know was that I felt just as bad for her as she did for me.

Although my goal for the day was to do well for Mom, I couldn't help but feel anxious. I felt healthy, so it was hard to consider that by the end of the day, I could be sick. I offered a quick prayer to the heavens: *Aunt Sue, please be with Mom and me. We need you. All the angels and saints, please pray for us.* And I'm pretty sure there was a Hail Mary mixed in there too.

I greeted everyone at the front counter, signed in, took a

seat, and waited all of about five minutes before hearing, "Miss Stachler? We're ready for you." My heart was pounding.

Mom was familiar with the routine from being here with Dad. It wasn't totally new to me either, so in that way the awful familiarity was comforting and reassuring to both of us. Mom sought out the perfect station for the day while I headed over to weigh in. The first nurse had me step on the scale and then took my heart rate, blood pressure, and temperature before sending me off to the next nurse's station to "tap my port"—the lingo for getting my IV in.

I went around a partition to a recliner and was greeted by a bubbly young nurse.

"Hi! I'm Courtney. I'll be getting your IV set up." She was so full of energy and exuded such an air of happiness that for a minute I forgot where I was.

She began by opening the bandage on the inside of my upper left arm, revealing the fresh one-inch incision from the surgery I had undergone two days earlier to get my port implanted. The cut was tender, puffy, and raw, and I began to worry about how much this was going to hurt. The skin hadn't fused closed yet, and I kept imagining it splitting opening.

Courtney told me to raise my arm, rest it above my head on the back of the recliner, and keep it as still as possible while she gently jabbed what felt like a nail-size needle through my skin into the new, round, almost doorbell-like button underneath it.

My port. Via this thing, the meds would travel through a soft, squishy tube into my arm, up around my shoulder, and down to my heart. From there, I was told the drugs would be dumped and dispersed throughout my body. The port would make it easier to draw blood and administer drugs, and it wouldn't be as harsh on my veins. All I knew was that I was starting to feel like a science experiment.

I let out an audible sigh of relief after the needle had been inserted. I'd been holding my breath because I was more nervous about this part hurting than anything else. For that moment, I was pleased with myself. I took it as a small success, and those small successes were what I learned to rely on along the way. Courtney continued chatting with me as she secured the needle with a large, clear sticker and a white gauze armband.

"You're all set," she said with a smile.

"Thanks so much," I said. "That really wasn't too bad. See you next time."

I strolled past recliners occupied by patients and their family members. I stood tall, smiling, taking it all in. I realize now that I probably looked like a fool—so new, so naive, so unaware. I clearly had "rookie" plastered across my face, and I didn't even know it. I saw tired patients, ill patients, worn-out patients. I wasn't like them—yet.

The stations were divided by movable partitions made of PVC pipes and blue canvas fabric. Each space had two oversize recliners in matching teal fabric facing a wall of windows, with a padded office chair in each corner, a wheelie stool, and a TV on a small stand. Mom had found us a quiet spot around the corner. I was relieved to see that we had the whole station to ourselves. Mom was already sitting in her chair.

As soon as she saw me, she asked, "Are you okay? They didn't hurt you, did they?"

I took my seat in the big recliner. "It didn't hurt. We're all good."

The nurse assigned to me for the day came over. Dana was calm and unassuming, which made me feel relaxed. While she was hooking up a bag of fluids and another bag of liquid chemicals, she explained how the day would progress.

"This is the first of the four different drugs you'll have today. Once this bag is empty, I'll get the next one set up. You'll have one at a time."

So that's it, I thought. *That's the stuff. It looks like water. There's no way this is going to make me sick.* I was listening to Dana but stopped paying much attention to what she was saying. I trusted her, so I didn't have any questions. I did tune back in when she mentioned the drug Adriamycin, which I'd have later in the day. I knew about that one. It's nicknamed the Red Devil. I remembered Dad saying, "That stuff's lethal." I guess anything with the word *devil* in it can't be good, but right then, it didn't seem like a big deal.

We were all set. Dana asked, "Are you comfortable?"

"Yes, thank you."

"Okay. Let me know if you need me. I'll be back later to check on you."

The new-patient excitement around me subsided—the waving, smiling, introductions, and chitchat had ended, and the nurses faded away. The room became still, and there we were—just Mom and I facing each other. Mom was studying my face, and I think we both winced as the first drop hit the IV tube.

I was proud of the momentum we'd kept up. Mom and I were each doing our part to hold it together for the other. I watched the slow drip of the IV, one drop at a time. And with each drop, I had a different thought. Drop one: *here we go.* Drop two: *I did it. See, it's nothing.* Drop three: *I don't feel anything.* Drop four: *I don't feel sick.* One drop into the tube, sliding down it and into me, and then the next drop. It was odd looking up at that bag of liquid and realizing that whatever was in there was going to make my cancer go away. My cure was floating in that plastic pouch.

All I had heard about that morning was how potentially ill this chemo could make me. The litany of side effects was endless, so I chose to block them out. Mom, knowing that the two of us couldn't just sit there in silence willing the time to pass, worked to distract me. She began sorting through the cooler next to her. "Let's see. What would you like to drink?"

"I'm fine right now."

"Hold on. I have Fresca, water, ginger ale, lemonade. What sounds good?"

"Mom, I'm really not that thirsty."

She seemed dejected. "You have to drink something. It'll help flush the drugs out. Please try a little something."

So I obliged. And, with that, Mom was in motion. She popped up the tray at the side of my recliner, opened my can of soda, and hurried off to grab a straw. She returned with not only a straw, but also a handful of wrapped candies and mints. As if offering me my choice of diamonds and jewels, Mom held out her hand. "What would you like? Peppermint? Cherry? Butterscotch?"

Staring at the colorful wrappers in Mom's palm, I realized that those candies and the variety of drinks were probably the only two things holding Mom together. I reached for the peppermint, and Mom was temporarily happy.

An hour later, I started to feel waterlogged and bloated. I was afraid that my worries were beginning to show on my face. I wiggled my shoulders and twisted my head from side to side, hoping that this would shake off the discomfort. I continued chatting (or, more accurately, nodding to prompt Mom to keep the conversation going). But I couldn't stop the thoughts running through my head. *Oh no. I think I feel weird.* I couldn't tell if it was just in my mind. *Am I feeling sick because everyone told me I would? Or am I becoming physically ill?* I wasn't sure.

I guess Mom must have seen me trying to fight off the initial effects. She got up, laid the fuzzy fleece blanket that she'd brought from home over me, and tucked it under my feet. "Honey, why don't you close your eyes and nod off for a bit? Let the medicine do its job."

Nod off? No. There was no way I was doing that. I wanted to stay in control. Besides, I wasn't going to leave Mom alone. If I was awake, she'd know I was fine. But the momentum we had kept up all morning wouldn't last much longer. I found myself looking back up at the bag, the liquid dripping slowly into the IV tube. Mom's talking stopped, and I felt her zero in on my face. I moved my eyes away from the IV pole and looked down at my hands, tightly clenched, resting in my lap. Mom had moved up next to me. She crouched down beside me and grasped my right hand. I wanted to say something, but I wasn't even sure what I was thinking.

"What is it, honey?"

My eyes filled with tears. "Nothing." I closed my eyes, hoping to direct my thoughts somewhere else. Mom waited patiently, and then in a quiet whisper, so low that only she could hear, I said, "I don't want to be here."

"I know," she replied.

A few tears streamed down my cheeks. "But I—"

"I know," she repeated, stopping me before I could say one more word. "I don't want you to be here either."

We made it to the afternoon, and as hard as it is to believe, I was excited to see Dana, with her rubber gloves on and a large syringe in her hand. I knew she was coming to give me more drugs, but I didn't care. It was time for the Red Devil, which she would have to slowly push through my port over the course of thirty minutes. Mom was relieved that a nurse was present to watch me and give her a moment's break, and I was secretly thankful that Dana was there to chat with Mom and give *me* a break. Dana sat on the low stool next to me, screwed the large syringe to the end of the tube dangling from my port, and began gently pressing the end of it. While she was talking with Mom, I watched in amazement and curiosity as the red concoction slowly made its way into my veins. I was told this drug was so toxic that if it touched my skin, I'd get third-degree burns. Yet there it was, going inside me. In a matter of minutes, I began to feel foggy, disconnected, and discouraged. Feeling myself slumping in the chair, I fought with all my might to stay focused and alert.

After all the drinks Mom had forced down me and the steady stream of drugs, it was inevitable that eventually I'd have to get up and make my way to the bathroom. I pushed in the recliner's footrest, and the back came forward. As soon as I stood up, I felt wobbly, nauseous, and unsteady. I swear, I could feel the drugs sloshing around inside me. My energy was zapped and my feet felt heavy. Mom put her arm around my waist as I grabbed the IV pole, and the two of us shuffled down the hall to the bathroom.

Reaching for the handle, Mom said, "Let me get the door."

The tile walls and wood door were the only things separating Mom and me, yet I felt terribly alone. In that tiny, cold, sterile bathroom, I didn't have to smile or put on an act or talk or anything. I just sat there. I didn't feel well. When I saw the fruit punch–colored pee in the toilet, I knew I was in trouble. I'd thought I could will away the side effects of the drugs, but I couldn't. I did as Dana had instructed, flushing the toilet twice, while marveling at the fact that this stuff was so poisonous that I had to flush the toilet *twice* before anyone else could enter. As I washed my hands, I studied my face in the mirror. Something was different. The girl in the reflection already seemed changed.

I opened the door to see Mom standing right where I left her. I gave her a very timid smile and a slight nod. The talking, the mindless conversations, the sodas and variety of snacks, her little trips to the candy bowl, were all to distract us from what was going on. But Mom knew what was really happening. Putting her arm around my waist again to help guide me back to my seat, she whispered, "You're doing a good job."

As discreetly as possible, I told her, "But, Mom, my pee was *red*." It was happening. I was sick.

.... ❧ ....

By the time we made it back into the car to head home, the drugs had taken over. I propped my head against the window as my insides began to shake. I stayed still, keeping my eyes closed as I listened to Mom repeat, "We're almost home. Hold on. We're almost there." She reached over to rest a hand on my leg. "I'm right here." That made my eyes tear up and my bottom lip quiver. Mom's touch was comforting. I knew that I needed her and that I would lean on her. I already had. And I despised this disease for making me do that.

When the two of us got home, we were already trapped in the world of chemo, managing our way through the side effects. I soon found that sitting in the chair at treatment was the least of it. The chemo hit me hard, much harder than Dr. Weens had anticipated.

The profuse sweating began immediately after treatment. I'd go straight to bed and crash, only to be awakened by my drenched T-shirt clinging to my back. Every pore in my body went into overdrive, trying to get rid of the liquid chemicals coursing through me. It was disgusting. My hair would be wet, and beads of sweat would roll down the backs of my legs. I was so weak that I was almost unable to cross the room to my dresser for a change of clothes.

I had expected the nausea. But even with the anti-this and anti-that drugs, I had horrible queasiness. My stomach flip-flopped and convulsed. Mom and I got good at our ice routine, pressing ice packs on my neck, down my back, and over my head to stop me from throwing up. It was necessary, but maddening.

The freezing cold would shock my system, lessening the need to vomit my guts out. I'd wait for it to get as bad as I could take, then I'd simply call out, "I'm not doing well." That was my cry for help. Within seconds, Mom would have frozen ice packs shoved onto my skin. I hated it. I tensed from the bitter cold, the gut-wrenching pain and sickness, but also from the fact that I needed her to do this for me. It would always end with me saying, "Mom, I'm trying. I am so sorry."

Then there was the tingling of my scalp as my hair began to fall out. My entire body became puffy from steroids, which also left me jumpy. I felt tired and weak, yet wired and awake. I didn't even know how that was possible, but it was. My vision became blurry, and I experienced alarming amnesia. I also had achy muscles and dry mouth.

I'd been told there was a minute chance that I could get a rare side effect: facial bone pain. And, of course, I did get it—horrifying pain in my bones. I was terrified, yelling, "It's my head, my eye sockets, my cheeks, my teeth, my chin, my jaw. Is this normal? What's happening?"

Mom was panicked too. "I don't know, honey. I don't know."

The pain was excruciating. "I can't take it!" I screamed. The only thing that helped slightly was applying pressure by gripping my face with both my hands. After an emergency phone call and following every possible recommendation from the doctors, I still couldn't get relief.

My days started to run together, and my life became confined to the couch and my bed. The future seemed daunting, and trying to think of the next day was, at times, more than I could do. I'd open my eyes reluctantly in the morning, hoping to make it to the afternoon, then to dinner, and so on. My days were divided into four-hour increments, from one pill to the next. Sometimes I just wanted it to be bedtime so I could take my sleeping pill. It was never good sleep and only lasted about five hours. The rest of the time, I was awake—fighting, feeling, dealing with it all. But at least I was not alone.

Mom became my full-on caretaker. She watched me around the clock, sleeping on the floor in my room, doling out pills at all hours of the day and into the night, keeping medicine charts and schedules, giving me the shots I needed, rubbing my back for hours hoping I'd nod off, and making snacks and buying different drinks, even though I would only be able to take one bite or one sip. She listened to any and all of my concerns, complaints, and fears. As the weeks and months went by, the chemo had a cumulative effect, and by the end, we were both sort of going through the motions. Chemo had become our full-time jobs— caretaker and patient. And I felt incredibly guilty. She had other things she should be doing, like working on her dessert business or helping the other kids or running the household.

Late one night, I laid awake in bed, clenching my pillow, hoping the pain would lessen. The sicker I got, the more afraid I became that I was failing. The weaker I grew, the scarier it was. *What's happening to the cancer? Is this stuff working?* Mom, sleeping on a pile of pillows and blankets on the floor, heard my pathetic whimpers and sat up next to me.

I whispered, "I'm not doing this well."

"Yes you are," she said.

"No I'm not. I had no idea. What about Dad? He wasn't this bad."

"Yes he was. He didn't want you kids to see."

Distressed, I asked, "What about Aunt Sue?"

"You're doing a good job," she insisted. "A really good job. She would be so proud of you."

The chemo also created what seemed like a permanent metallic taste in my mouth, as if I were constantly licking an aluminum can. That was compounded by the rotten taste that rose from my throat and lingered on my tongue—that atrocious taste alone was enough to make me nauseous. My taste buds had gone wacky too. I craved anything with a strong flavor that might give me a temporary release from these awful tastes. I'd ask Mom, "Can I have bacon?" only to be able to eat one bite.

The worse my symptoms were, the more upset I became. It only happened once, but I won't forget the time that I was so worn out that I called Mom to my room to talk. "What are my odds?" I asked her. "What would happen if we stopped all of this?"

When it dawned on her what I was asking, she was furious.

"I am telling you—you *need* this treatment!" Of course, I wasn't really going to stop chemo. I just wanted to pretend for a minute that I could if I wanted to.

I was lucky I had no commitments other than getting well. That was my sole purpose. Thanks to my parents, I was afforded the luxury of being able to sleep, lie around, watch TV, and do nothing—but that wasn't always easy. I had no work, no career, no apartment, no place of my own, no bills, no rent. I sold my car. I had very little money. I had graduated college, and now I was stuck in this terrible limbo. As thankful as I was that my only job was to get through treatment, it was also hard feeling like I didn't have anything really going for me. Sometimes I felt like a little kid who needed her mom; other times, I just felt old.

One afternoon, I traded my bed for the couch in the family room. I was trying to watch TV (*Oprah* at four o'clock was part of our daily routine), but I'd taken a slew of pills that made me doze off. I woke up to see Mom standing over me with a tray of hot cookies. They smelled great, but I wasn't sure why she had brought the whole tray in. Holding it out to me, she said, "Don't these look nice? I thought they might sound good to you. Want to try one?"

I'd never seen her bake these cookies before. They were little, light-brown cookies with sugar on top that sparkled almost like glitter. Not one of Mom's usual elaborate creations. So I said, "Well, I don't know. What are they?"

"They're gingersnaps. Just try one."

The aroma was enticing, so I took a bite. The cookie was crunchy and light. The flavors were warm and comforting—cinnamon, ginger, and cloves. It melted in my mouth, and I could actually taste it, which was never a given these days, considering my whacked-out taste buds. It was delicious.

Dear Sue,

I didn't like leaving the house when Ken or Susan were sick, but there were occasions when I had to run a quick errand. I'd wait until someone else was home.

I was at the post office, happy to stand quietly in line for a few minutes—a few minutes of peace. Soon, there was one person in line behind me, then two. Apparently they didn't know each other, but they became fast friends, mutually grumbling, "Look at this line. Will you look at how inefficient they are here? There is always a wait."

I looked back, thinking, Must you? Do you really have to complain?

They mistook my interest and prompted me to join them. "Don't you think this is ridiculous?"

The employees were aware by now of the unwarranted criticism, and although I tried, the glares I directed at these two weren't stopping them. I started to get annoyed. I couldn't help but think of the hundreds of people I'd seen come and go through Dr. Weens's office over the years who would have loved a chance to be out and about, running an ordinary errand. Not to mention the girl I had left at home on my couch.

Soon there was another comment. "These postal workers can see all of us waiting, and they're not making the slightest effort." I wasn't just irritated by the remarks now; I was also embarrassed and didn't want the employees to think that my place in line put me in cahoots with these two loudmouths.

As my transaction was pleasantly and efficiently completed, my anger got the better of me. Sue, you won't believe what I did! I made a split-second decision, thinking, I'll show those two, *and I spun around. "Excuse me, there," I began, addressing them directly. "How dare you stand there and complain, criticizing these hardworking people?"*

Imagine my surprise when I saw that the two-person line I'd intended to speak to had become a whole host of people lined up out the door! But I was already too committed to my speech to stop. "Don't you have anything better to do with your time than pick on people who are doing their jobs? You should be ashamed of yourselves for your petty complaining. Can't you think of something more useful to do?"

Remember how I'd always turn bright red whenever I was nervous or embarrassed? I'm sure I was red then, but I didn't care. Although I have to admit that as I marched out the door, I was relieved that I didn't know anyone in that line! Complaining over nothing? You never did. I realized that day that Susan wasn't the only one who had changed; I had too.

7

Cancer Buddies

THE SUMMER BEFORE I WAS DIAGNOSED, DAD WENT through an extensive chemo regimen, and he still had to have "maintenance" treatments every few months. I'm almost sure that Dr. Weens didn't describe it that way, but that's what we called it. Even in his worst moments, Dad never let on to how bad the chemo made him feel. He would go to treatments on Fridays, stay in his bedroom for three days, and then somehow pull himself together enough to put on a suit, go to work, and resume a "normal" routine. He carried on with a sense of humor and lived each day by not letting cancer define him. Even now, it's almost like Dad doesn't even know he has cancer, because he doesn't acknowledge it.

That's why I was so upset about Dad being "let go." As if chemo weren't enough to deal with, Dad was blindsided at work, twice. He met with Dr. Weens on a Friday and was told he needed chemo, then he went into the office and told his boss. Returning the next Monday, Dad was demoted on the spot after holding the same position and title for twenty years. I hated that he was being treated that way. His work ethic is unparalleled, and besides, he would only miss a handful of days while going through treatment. A few months later, he was let go due to "restructuring." I remember going with my family to help him clean out his office. I happened to see Dad consoling a sweet custodian who was in tears over him being let go. Dad has a way of making everyone around him feel at ease. He never makes anything about him, and he's genuinely interested in others. Within two minutes of meeting someone, Dad will essentially know where they were born, which sports teams they root for, and the names of their kids or pets. It doesn't matter if it's the janitor or the CEO, he finds something in common with them. What I saw my dad do with the custodian that day was one of his finest moments.

Dad losing his job was also why I felt extra horrible walking through the back gate in March after the nurse found the lump on my neck. It wasn't like Dad could just go out and get a new job right then, because he was still in treatment himself. So Mom and Dad began talking about what they were going to do. We ate dinner as a family regularly, so this was a frequent topic of conversation around the table. Sometimes we mused about opening a piña colada hut in the Caribbean, or we talked more seriously about Dad starting his own CPA practice. Mom had a teaching degree but had become a stay-at-home mom when my older brother, Robert, was born, and had never gone back to teaching. So when Mom first said, "I'm thinking about maybe baking some cakes to sell," I thought, *Oh, great, go for it!* But I also thought, *How many cakes can Mom really bake and sell from the kitchen?*

When Mom called me at school months later and said, "I'm moving forward with the dessert business," I certainly didn't laugh, but I couldn't quite picture how it would work. Even so, I was enthusiastic and ready to help with whatever she needed.

Eventually, friends started hearing about Mom's endeavor and, while the business was small, Mom was staying busy. She had always enjoyed baking in the midst of the commotion at home. She could get lost in her kitchen. It was a nice diversion, and I think Dad knew that too.

My parents always made time for us, and there was nothing Dad wouldn't do for one of his kids. He might have had a stressful corporate schedule, but he was available. Dad never missed anything that was important to me. When I took art classes or drama, he showed an interest. He taught me how to rake the front yard, change a tire, and sharpen a good pencil for the SATs. Chemo was not on the agenda.

Dad didn't know that while he was going through treatment, he was setting an example I would come to rely on just a few months later. I wasn't nearly as scared as one might think, because Dad made cancer, treatment, appointments, and testing look normal. Maybe getting cancer and going through treatment should have been extra scary because Dad had just done it, but it was the opposite. Dad and I had the same surgeon, doctors, nurses, and oncologist, and we went to the same cancer center and hospital. It was physically difficult for Dad to watch me in treatment. He knew what was happening, exactly how it felt, the sickness and pain I was experiencing. I'd ask, "Did that happen to you?" and he'd usually respond, "Yes." In those moments, it was nice to know that I wasn't imaging things; he made me feel normal. But beyond that, we didn't talk much about cancer.

When I went with my parents to my first appointment with Dr. Weens, as soon as we'd walked through the entrance, Johnny, the welcoming receptionist, called out, "Mr. Stachler, it's nice to see you!" Then, perplexed, he asked, "But what are you doing here? I didn't see your name on the books."

Dad greeted Johnny warmly, saying, "I'm not here for me. I'd like you to meet my daughter, Susan."

The smile dropped from Johnny's face. "I'm so sorry."

"It's okay," I chimed in quickly. "Do I sign in here?"

I think we surprised them at the front desk. A father-daughter cancer duo… It's not exactly common. But standing next to Dad, I felt at ease. I was proud of him, or rather, I was proud to be his daughter. Looking around, I noticed some patients in the waiting room who seemed grumpy. I realized then that I had a choice. I could choose how I would act. Dad had incurable cancer, but he always chose to smile.

Watching Dad at my first appointment, I knew that I wanted others to see me like they saw him. I would smile, be kind and thoughtful, even when I felt sick and miserable or had bad days. He made it look easy by choosing to have an upbeat, positive attitude, by not making it about himself, by smiling even when he didn't want to. Dad's had a lot on his shoulders, but you'd never know it. That is a true hero. That takes a certain inner strength and quiet courage. I don't know if I always succeeded, but I tried my very best to be just like him.

Dear Sue,

After you died, I made a bargain with the heavens. I didn't want anything bad to happen to anyone I loved, but I hoped that, at least, there'd be no more cancer. It was terrible watching you suffer. Ken and I were both forty-one years old when we were told that he had lymphoma. I couldn't believe it. Our children, your nieces and nephews, were so young. Not only was I completely aware of what Ken was up against, but I thought I'd lose him, like I lost you.

I don't need to tell you how brutal chemo is. Forget your cancer, the treatment alone nearly killed you many times over. I've wondered more times than I can count what it took for you to keep living for as long as you did. And the older I become, the more I'm awed by your bravery.

I'm not the only one who has wondered. One afternoon, when Ken was three months into chemo, he was as sick as I've ever seen him. He was in bed, curled up on his side. I approached him quietly, wanting to make sure that he was still sleeping and trying not to wake him. He shifted slightly, and his eyes opened slowly. Faintly, he said, "Hi."

I knelt down next to him and reached to grasp his hands in mine. The fun-loving guy you knew, the guy with more energy than anyone I've ever known, was leveled. Distressed, I asked, "Are you still in there?" I needed to make sure that he was trying as hard as he could. I needed him to get through treatment and come back to me, the "old" Ken.

He took a slow, deep breath and assured me, "I'm here." Then he whispered, "I was just thinking about Sue. How in God's name did she do this?" Sue, I don't know how you withstood what was done to you. And I didn't know whether to be comforted that Ken was thinking of you or...alarmed.

I tried to soothe him. "No one could do this any better than you."

"Laura." Ken paused. "What if this happens...to one of the kids?"

"Oh, Ken," I said, startled. "The kids are all fine." I couldn't imagine where that had come from. Leave it to Ken to be thinking, right then, about our children. Trying to ease his unfounded concern, I promised, "Nothing is going to happen to them."

I adjusted his covers, in a weak attempt to comfort him, and kissed his cheek. He faded back to sleep. We never mentioned it again.

8

Dueling Patients

WHEN WE FOUND OUT THAT DAD AND I WOULD BE having chemo on the same day, I weirdly started looking forward to it. I wasn't happy that Dad had cancer or that he needed treatment, of course, but since he did, I thought, *Well, let's do this together.* All three of us—Mom, Dad, and me. I thought having Dad sit next to me would be kind of nice. It was like "bring your dad to work day," or something like that, and I figured I'd get through the day riding on the coattails of Dad's gregarious personality and sense of humor.

After getting my port tapped, I came to our station and saw one of our favorite nurses, Cindy, quietly talking with Mom. She held Mom's hands in hers and said, "Laura, I woke up today thinking about you and your family. And I prayed for you. We're going to take good care of Ken and Susan. But I want you to know that we are here for you too. We're going to help you get through this day."

Cindy had taken care of Dad many times before and had gotten to know my parents over the past year. She was one of the few people who knew not only about Dad and me, but also about Aunt Sue. Hearing Cindy comfort my mom, my heart just about broke. I knew Dad and I would be fine, but what about Mom?

We nestled into our recliners and popped the footrests up. Looking up at his IV pole, Dad asked me, "Want to make a bet?"

"About what?"

"Who's going to finish first today. I bet I win!"

Cheerfully, I asked, "What do I get if I win?"

"An extra candy from the bowl. Come on, take your best guess. Pick a time!"

By then I was laughing. "Dad, those candies are free. I can have as many as I want."

Mom joined in. "Ken! Stop it!" But she was clearly tickled.

With that, Dad stretched out and glanced over at Mom. "Hon, I'll see you a little later," he said and closed his eyes. That was the end of it. The silliness and chatter stopped. It turned out that Dad did chemo differently than I expected. Rather than joke his way through it, he simply checked out. The day ended up being nothing special—I just had chemo alongside my sleeping dad while Mom watched over us.

The only slightly fun part of the day was sharing a few of Mom's cookies with the other patients, which I had started doing over the past few months. I'd stop by a few recliners in the morning when I got there, before I got hooked up for the day, saying, "I brought you some gingersnaps. Enjoy!" or "My mom made these. I thought you might like them."

Most people were surprised and happy to get a little treat on what would prove to be, in most cases, a miserable day. "These are for me? How sweet of you."

We didn't leave the nurses and staff out either. I'd share samples of cakes and new cheesecake flavors that Mom was working on for her business—and some cookies too. It wasn't uncommon for a nurse to say, "Are you the one who left us the cake?" or "Thank you for the goodies! We loved them! They were gone by the afternoon."

A few nurses knew what Mom was trying to do with her bakery, and they were sincerely interested. It meant a lot to me when a nurse would talk with Mom, asking how she was or how things were going with the bakery.

Of course, the nurses knew that ginger helps settle stomachs, so once they'd caught wind of Mom's cookies, they asked if she'd be willing to bring individual packets of them for patients undergoing chemo. They suggested that she make a flyer too. "You know the days here get long," one nurse commented. "This will give people something new to look at."

The morning that Dad and I had chemo together, I walked in with a basket filled with ziplock bags of gingersnaps and a sign that we'd printed out at home advertising Mom's business. She didn't want anyone to feel obligated to her—the cookies were really just meant for people to enjoy. But I set the cookies on the front counter, pinned her flyer to the bulletin board right above it, and placed a few business cards nearby, hoping that someone would call her for an order.

Dear Sue,

Ken had nodded off at chemo, and I was grateful that Susan decided to as well. Their IVs were dispensing, and I was left sitting there, trusting that stuff to work. Quickly, I grabbed a home decorating magazine to distract myself before I broke down. I had to have faith that I'd be forgiven for not praying for them in that moment. It was one of the saddest things I've ever seen, the two of them lying there.

That morning, Susan had brought some of my cookies to the hospital to share. I wasn't sure if her fellow patients would like the gingersnaps I'd made or not, but I had a feeling that they'd welcome her thoughtful gesture. I wasn't wrong. Her smile and heartfelt comments only endeared her to them more. Like you had been, she was decades younger than most of the patients. Shoot, she could have been giving away those seventies-style macramé plant holders we used to make (wooden beads optional), and they would've been delighted! It was amazing to see how the patients' demeanors changed during their brief exchanges with Susan.

As for the gingersnaps? I only hoped they would be able to enjoy the cookies, if they felt well enough to try them.

9

Nuke It!

THE FINAL NEEDLE WAS OUT, THE MONTHS OF CHEMO were over. Tears of joy and tears of exhaustion streamed down my face. *How did we do this? And now what?* Shaking my head in disbelief, I looked to Mom for confirmation. She said, "All done, honey. You're all done." I felt an unexpected sense of sadness. Mom and I had gotten so used to showing up, doing chemo, and navigating the days in between. It wasn't easy, and I wanted it to be over, but on the other hand, Mom and I had learned what to anticipate, and we had both worked to be "good" at it.

Occasionally, I'd go out with Randy or with friends, but over time, I left the house less and less. I would become physically tired when I went out, but more than that, it was the emotional drain that I didn't care for. I didn't want people looking at me, because I could see the questions on their faces: *How'd you get cancer? What did you do wrong?* I sensed some people worried about themselves, wondering what they could do to prevent ending up like me. I was also shy about the cancer. I was quietly doing my thing, and I wanted to keep it that way. I didn't want to answer questions. I appreciated the simple, "Thinking of you." That said it all, and I didn't need much more than that. There generally aren't too many people in their early twenties with cancer, and the bandanna around my head was an unfortunate giveaway that made it hard to fly under the radar.

Sometimes I'd have lunch at our local Mexican restaurant with my nineteen-year-old brother Luke, going late, when it was less crowded. We'd eat cheese dip and sit in a booth until Luke had not only devoured his plate of food, but finished mine too. It wasn't until later that I found out Mom had given him the cash to take me to lunch! Early on, Carey and I tried to go shopping. (Mom would follow along behind us with an empty wheelchair, "Just in case you need it." Eventually, I did.) Then we decided that our time together would be best spent at home, watching Julia Roberts movies on repeat. Stephanie, my best friend since first grade, flew in from San Francisco to visit, and even then we were stuck inside, watching TV while she modeled the wig that I never ended up using. We laughed so hard until we cried together. Anastasia, another close friend, would pick me up for dinner now and then. We'd go to Chili's—always Chili's. Looking back, I realized that Chili's was the closest restaurant to our house. I'm sure she was worried that I would get tired and need to get home quickly.

Randy came around when he could, but he was in another state, having taken a summer job in Mississippi. I wanted to see him, but at the same time, I didn't want him to see me as sick as I was. Just as he was protective of me, I was protective of him. He was being incredibly supportive—one time he even drove all night to see me for only forty-five minutes before he had to drive back to work—but still, he hadn't signed up for this.

My brother Robert, who had also gone to Auburn, invited me out to my alma mater to tailgate and go to a football game with his friends one Saturday. I went, but it was not my smartest move. It was fun, in theory, but as the day went on, I grew fatigued. I felt like a bozo sitting in a camping chair, having my brother wait on me (which he insisted on doing). I don't know if I was physically exhausted or if I was just worn out from all the looks and constant questions.

Although seeing people was exhausting, I liked talking on the phone, and my calls with Randy or close friends became the highlight of my day. But even then, if the person I was talking to asked how I was feeling, I'd say, "Let's talk about something else. Tell me what's going on with you." On a bad day, at least I could still fake it on the phone.

.... ❧ ....

The next step in my treatment was what I considered the easy part—radiation therapy. As I understood it, I'd be zapped daily with a powerful x-ray machine that would burn off any leftover cancer cells that hadn't been killed during chemo. I'd had a broken arm x-rayed before, and that was nothing, so I wasn't concerned about this part of the treatment. Besides, Dr. Cline, my radiation oncologist, had an unruffled, cool composure. His demeanor alone diminished any worries that I might have had.

On my first day of radiation, I found myself happily greeting the receptionist. "Hi! We're here—Susan Stachler." I don't know when I started doing this, but I heard myself say "we." I didn't want to be alone through any part of this, and I didn't want Mom to feel left out either. We were in this together.

Mom became "my person." She almost always knew what I was thinking, always stuck up for me, and was always tough and unwavering, even at moments when it must have been incredibly difficult. Being the caretaker is its own gig, and it's not an easy task. There were plenty of times I was happier being me, rather than being in my mom's shoes, even though I was the one with cancer.

This place was bright and fresh, with glass walls and an aquarium in the middle. But the atmosphere was glum. Mom and I were making small talk when a technician came to the waiting room. "Susan? We're ready for you" she said, looking directly at Mom.

"I'm not Susan," Mom responded, looking distressed. This had happened a few times.

"Mom, it's okay." I hopped out of my chair and gathered up my things. Mom was sensitive to the fact that she wasn't the patient.

The technician showed me into a dark room with all kinds of equipment and a table in the middle. My therapy was going to be in the area of my neck, throat, and chest, so I had to lie faceup on the table, naked from the waist up, with my head placed in a doughnut-shaped pillow and my chin tilted back. There were two technicians, one on each side of me, and they adjusted me until my body lay exactly where they needed it. The technicians were doing specific calculations, and I was fascinated but uneasy, feeling like a turtle on its back—defenseless. This treatment was very precise, and every millimeter had to be accounted for.

The technicians took multiple imaging scans and measurements using a ruler of some sort, red laser beams, and bright lights. They were concentrating so hard on their jobs that there was no time for conversation or banter, and while I appreciated the attention they were paying to the process, I felt like Cancer Patient Number 146. It was like they temporarily forgot there was a person under the black marker they were using to outline exactly where the radiation should be targeted.

I stayed as still as possible, following the technicians' instructions. But when they moved my head, my bandanna slipped, which upset me. No one had seen my head without my bandanna. I had barely even looked at it, but I knew that my hair had thinned considerably, and my head was bald in patches. I would wake up every morning, grab the bandanna, wrap it around my head, and secure it with a knot at the base of my neck before I even sat up. I desperately wanted to cry out, "Please, please, stop. I need to fix something." And although this process—the scans and measurements—didn't hurt physically, my self-esteem was bruised. This was a level of vulnerability I had never experienced before.

Just as I was about to speak up, one of the technicians, who was drawing the final line across my chin and who Mom and I would forever refer to as Marking Pen Lady, asked, "Are you the one who brought the orange chocolate chip cookies?"

Could this get more awkward? I thought. "Yes," I answered. "My mom baked them."

"Those were delicious."

"My mom will be so happy to hear that you liked them."

"I heard she runs a bakery," the technician said. "Before you leave, I'd like to place an order. What else does your mom bake? Do you have a menu on you?"

Well, considering I was half-naked on a table, no. I didn't have a brochure or menu on me, but I was ready to go tell Mom that she had a new customer.

Once they completed the process, I was scrambling to fix my bandanna and put my clothes back on when the technician motioned to my head and said, "You can go across the street to the women's center, and they can do something for that."

I suppose she was trying to be helpful, but her remark was so bold, and I already felt exposed. But I managed to remain composed and squeaked out, "Thank you. See you tomorrow. I'll bring a menu with me."

As I left, I decided that I'd get better at this. I promised myself that I would never feel this way again during my radiation. I'd get better at training myself to "escape," to not feel vulnerable.

On the way to the car, I said, "Mom, guess what? There are a few people in the back who are interested in ordering from you. They want me to bring in a menu."

The treatment process had been such an upsetting experience that I chose not to describe it to Mom. I couldn't even tell her what the technician had said to me about my hair. By that point, if anyone had even looked at me wrong, Mom would have been livid. It would be years before I shared with her what had happened. For now, I spent the car ride home staring out the window, too mortified to say a word.

.... ❧ ....

Have you ever seen the movie *Groundhog Day*? That's what going to radiation came to feel like as I repeated the process over and over. Greet the receptionist and chat like I hadn't just seen her the day before; sign in; wait in the lobby and stare at the pretty fish tank; go to the locker room to change my clothes; head into the large, dark, cold room with a mammoth machine that zapped me from above; then flip over so it could zap me from the back. The only thing that changed was my throat became more and more burned with each treatment. The zapping was painless, but afterward, it would start to hurt, a burning, unrelenting pain.

The only way I could get through it was to turn it into a game. I hated dropping my hospital gown and being naked on the cold table while the technicians positioned me. I found it funny that they wore protective aprons and left the room to stand shielded behind a thick glass wall while the machine blasted my bare skin.

Over the intercom, I heard, "Are you comfortable? Let us know if you need us."

That made me laugh. Not wanting to move a muscle, I called out, "I'm good. Thank you." The more time they'd spend making me "comfortable," the more uncomfortable I would become. I'll admit I had one constant worry, which seemed to be more pronounced when I was alone, trapped with my thoughts, staring at the machine above me: *How does this work? And is it working on me?* I learned to breathe and stay calm, and I trained my mind to escape. Sometimes I'd go to the beach, in my imagination, or to Old Town, San Diego, or to a Braves baseball game with Randy.

Once the radiation was over, no matter how I felt, I would return to the waiting room all smiles, desperate to hold it together for Mom.

At home, Mom was filling any orders she was able to get, but, in part because I was taking up so much of her time, she wasn't drumming up a whole lot of business. She liked spending time in her bakery though, and she would work on tweaking recipes in the garage whenever she had a few minutes to spare. Sometimes this experimentation resulted in an abundance of baked goods in our house. That wasn't a bad thing, except that swallowing had become a challenge for me. Mom liked having a reason to bake, so she would tell me about the people she had chatted with in the waiting room during my treatment that day and then ask, "If I bake some gingersnaps, will you bring them tomorrow?"

Soon we started bringing gingersnaps regularly to share with anyone who happened to be in the waiting room. It was great to see the reaction the cookies brought—people were smiling in a place where, frankly, there wasn't much to smile about. I never said much, just handed out bags of cookies. It felt good to have something to do.

It was lucky my treatment coincided with the upcoming holidays, which garnered a few sales for Mom. It turned out that my Marking Pen Lady had placed a sizable order for a family party, buying all sorts of cakes and cookies. Mom was happy to sell anything, but her recipes were formulated for large quantities, so when she only sold one dozen cookies out of a batch of three dozen, that wasn't ideal. Mom didn't want to have to mess with figuring out how to divide an egg in half. When Marking Pen Lady ordered several different flavors, Mom had too many leftovers. I had taken a few business classes and knew this was not a good return on her investment! But Mom enjoyed baking, and the stress relief it gave her was priceless, even if she was losing money as she tried to grow her business. Not wanting to appear like she was wheeling and dealing in the waiting room, she always brought extras for the patients, along with the paid deliveries she started bringing to the staff who were supporting her business.

Because we went to radiation treatments daily, we saw the same people in the waiting room all the time, and their reaction to my mom's treats was consistently incredible. It was amazing how such a little thing could make such a big difference to people. I don't know if it was the cookies themselves, the act of giving them away, or something else, but it definitely felt like something special was happening in that sad little waiting room.

Dr. Cline said my treatment would be finished the week of Thanksgiving, and Mom and I marked the date on the calendar, counting down the days. My throat hurt so badly I could barely eat, but I was hungry, and I could almost taste my favorite side dishes and Mom's pecan pie, which would taste even sweeter knowing that my treatments were over. But with each treatment I had, the burning sensation in my throat got worse—so much so that Mom made an extra appointment for me with Dr. Cline. I was in bad shape.

Dr. Cline asked, "How bad is it, Susan?"

"It hurts some," I answered.

Mom jumped in. "It doesn't hurt *some*. Susan is in

terrible pain. She can't even get down the numbing medicine you prescribed."

The radiation regimen I was on didn't allow for breaks, but Dr. Cline decided it would be best to postpone my next treatment for a few days. The skin on my throat had become scaly on the outside, and whatever peach-fuzz hair I'd had left on the back of my head had burned off. I could barely speak, which was tricky when I wanted to chat with my friends at radiation or give cookies away, and it hurt to swallow even my own spit.

While I was trying my best to get through the last few treatments, Mom was putting extra effort into Thanksgiving. Who knew so many conversations could be had about candle colors and vegetable casseroles! She worked to put together a pretty table, delicious food, and homemade pies. My whole family gathered around the table, talking and eating, happy that we were all together and that I was nearly done with treatments. I took a couple bites of mashed potatoes, but I couldn't swallow. I couldn't believe it—of everything on the table, mashed potatoes were the easiest food to eat, and I couldn't even get that down. I know it was irrational, but I was embarrassed my brothers and sister had to see me like that. *What must they be thinking?* I lowered my head, hoping no one would notice I was upset, and tried not to cry. This was supposed to be a celebration, and I felt like I was ruining it.

Suddenly, Mom got up and left the table. She returned

with a little box and handed it to me. I opened it and found a pretty sterling-silver charm bracelet inscribed with my initials and a message: "Courage with a Smile. Love, Your Family." I lost it. I had just been on the verge of crying over mashed potatoes… I didn't deserve this gift.

"Thank you so much," I said, barely able to get the words out. Everything—my frustration with the long treatment regimen, the pain I had been enduring, my fear and exhaustion—all came to a head at that moment. I started to cry.

Mom came around the table and gave me a gentle hug. "Let me help you put it on, Susan." Her touch was the most soothing thing I had felt in days.

Dear Sue,

Memories of you carrying your green throat-spray bottle around the house came back to me as I drove to the pharmacy to buy the same stuff for Susan, hoping it would help ease her pain a little. It didn't work for her, just like it didn't work for you. You had excruciating pain, and while Susan did her best not to let on, I know she did too. I couldn't fix it. It was devastating.

And while all this was going on, could I have been doing anything more ridiculous than baking cookies? Probably not. But I had bought a giant stainless steel mixer for my big kitchen in the garage, and the only thing I could do to distract Susan a little was bake. I'd insist that she bring cookies for the people I'd meet in the waiting room while she got zapped every day. So that's what we did. I bought ingredients at the grocery store (I didn't know how or where to buy wholesale) and baked dozens of cookies, and Susan gave them away. Her fellow patients liked them, and more importantly, they were distracted for a few minutes each day, and so was Susan. It wasn't anything much, but it was nice, and it worked. It was one little thing I could do.

One particular day, there was a nice older gentleman in the radiation lobby, sitting in a wheelchair, his wife next to him. Susan and I sat down near them and began chatting. I asked the gentleman how he was getting along. The couple described the side effects of his therapy—fatigue and terrible weakness. Although visibly disheartened, they were trying to stay optimistic. He was very sick. They wanted to know which of us was there for treatment, and, of course, it surprised them that Susan, my young, beautiful daughter, was the one who was sick.

A few minutes later, the nurse called Susan back. As she walked away, Susan turned to us, smiled, and gave me that look of hers—the one that said, It's all right, Mom. Don't worry.

I waved and said, "I'll be right here," just as I did every day. As Susan disappeared down the hall and around the corner, I looked at the older couple and shrugged.

The gentleman commented, "She's just so young, but at least she seems to be doing very well with her cancer." Then he added, "I hope one day, when I am not in pain, I can smile like your daughter."

I sighed. "She is in pain. Terrible pain... But she smiles anyway."

The sweeter she was, the more it hurt me.

The Driveway
Commute

TREATMENT WAS OVER, AND I WAS BEHIND IN LIFE.
At least, I was behind in what I believed that I, as a college graduate, should be doing. I felt an urgency to figure out what I was going to do next, but even though my treatment was over, I still didn't feel or look like myself. It was maddening. I had expected to start feeling well again right away, but what I didn't realize was I would not bounce back that quickly. No one, not Dr. Weens or Dr. Cline or any of the nurses we met along the way, had warned me about this. Recovery would be a gradual process—and let's just say patience isn't my forte. I had a bunch of checkup appointments and follow-up scans lined up, but I wanted to fill my days with something productive. Luckily, Mom had anticipated that I'd find this unstructured time frustrating.

One day when I was tired of hanging around the house, she

casually asked, "When you feel like it, do you want to come out to the shop?" She was trying to make me feel useful, and it worked. I felt so much better knowing that, even if I couldn't go out and get a job yet, I could at least help Mom a little with her business. I could let myself off the hook. Going to her bakery felt like getting out of the house, but I could always sit down if I felt tired or go back inside and lie down on the couch. With just a few weeks until Christmas (my favorite holiday), I decided not to stress or overthink things too much. I'd allow myself to enjoy December and then reevaluate in January.

With the holidays upon us, Mom received a fair number of dessert orders. Baked goods and the holidays just seem to go hand in hand. People needed sweets for their family get-togethers, office celebrations, cocktail parties, and cookie swaps. I'd never heard of a cookie swap before, but customers would ask Mom, "Do you mind leaving the label off the box? I don't want my friends to know I didn't bake them!" She would oblige, but then they'd taste one and say, "I don't know why I had you do that. No one is going to believe I baked these cookies. They're too good!"

People came to Mom's shop enthusiastic and ready to buy the perfect desserts to complete their holiday experience. She had struggled to solicit orders before, but now the hustle and bustle of the holiday season and people coming in and out made the shop lively and fun to be around. Word of mouth had spread, and she had a steady flow of customers. I got in the habit of going to the shop in the morning, when few customers came, because I was reluctant to be seen by strangers or have to answer their questions. And, really, I didn't want Mom to have to do that either. People had a way of putting her on the spot, asking her about me as if I weren't standing right there.

I wasn't able to help Mom much in the shop, but it gave me somewhere to go, and I liked that. Mom said I made her nervous, just standing there watching her, and she'd push me to sit down and get comfortable. I'd sit cross-legged on top of the front counter, which was a steel baking table with a solid butcher-block top. It was a family heirloom from Carver's, the pie-and-burger restaurant that her parents had owned in LA. I would sit there, chat with Mom, and sometimes put labels on boxes. It was neat seeing the labels in print, hundreds of them on a roll, since I had created the design.

When Mom was first starting her business, she called me at school and said, "So I was thinking… I need a logo for my bakery. What about one of your drawings?"

Pleased but surprised, I asked, "You want one of my little sketches? Are you sure?"

"You don't have to if you don't want to," Mom said, "but I'd love that."

I didn't see myself as an artist, although I spent hours drawing what my high school art teacher had deemed "flat, dull stick figures," but I sketched out a logo for Mom. It was kind of incredible now to see my work applied to hundreds of boxes of my mom's baked goods.

Although I avoided the shop during the day when it was busy, it was exciting to look out the window and see people pulling up the driveway to pick up cakes, cookies by the dozen, and tins of gingersnaps. Somehow, even in the midst of caring for Dad and me when we were sick, Mom had found the time and energy to make one of her own dreams come true. I was prouder of her than I could say.

.... ❧ ....

January came, and on my first "official" day of work in the shop, I found myself turning off the buzzer on my alarm, sliding out of bed, and pulling on my new uniform—sweatpants, a T-shirt, and sneakers. I headed down the hallway, stepped out the side door of the house, and walked across the driveway toward the garage. As I made the twenty-foot commute from our house to Mom's shop, I couldn't help but think, *It wasn't supposed to go like this.* I'd had an idea of what I'd do after college, and this was not it. Where was my black suit? I couldn't even remember if it was hanging in my closet, or if Mom had packed it away somewhere.

I was grateful to have something to do that would take my mind off what I'd been going through, even if it was only for a few hours a day. But when Mom asked me about officially working with her in her bakery, she was so enthusiastic that I immediately said yes, without even thinking about it. Now I was having second thoughts.

As I reached for the knob on the glass door to the bakery, I tried to reassure myself that everything was going to be okay. I was weak, worn out, and still recovering from my cancer treatments, and I knew that, for now, working with Mom was my only option. There was no way any employer would take a chance on hiring me while I was in this condition. Just look at what had happened to Dad the year before.

So there I was inside my new office—a four-hundred-square-foot bakeshop that had formerly been our family's garage. I used to store my Rollerblades where a three-foot mixer now sat. My brothers, sister, and I used to have an oversize tub of basketballs that had been replaced by a sink mounted on the wall. Dad used to park his lawn mower where a commercial-grade monster of an oven was now situated. Looking at it now, you would never know this cute little space had ever been a grungy garage. The floor was freshly painted, and the window frames and wood trim were a bright, cheerful red. We had even stenciled fun black polka dots on the white walls, to match the cute packaging Mom wrapped her creations in. I didn't know who was going to find Mom's shop on our quiet neighborhood street, at the top of our long driveway, but it looked adorable.

I stood apprehensively beside the stainless steel worktable in the middle of the shop as Mom finished frosting a three-layer cake. *What am I supposed to be doing?* As she whipped frosting with a spatula in her left hand and spun the cake pedestal with her right, I began to feel totally inadequate and unprepared. I was not a baker or a pastry chef or any sort of culinary expert. I wasn't even a business major. I figured I could probably build a few gift boxes, tally the orders, and sprinkle some sugar on the gingersnap cookies that were becoming Mom's bestseller. At least I knew one thing for certain: having Mom as a boss was going to be convenient. There were still days when I felt completely exhausted. Where else would I be able to come to work late, leave early, and essentially wear pajamas all the time?

Although I wasn't unhappy working with Mom, it didn't feel like a "real" job. At the most random times, while I'd be on the phone with a customer or watching Mom take a new batch of cookies out of the oven, I would find myself wondering, *What does it all mean? Who am I now? Where do I go from here?* I wished I could just move on or flip a switch that would let me forget everything I had been through over the past several months, but I couldn't. I was a different girl from the one who had crossed the stage at graduation, and I wasn't sure how to move forward.

That first day, as Mom popped the layer cake in the refrigerator, she called out a baking tip to me. "The cold air helps the frosting set."

Oh, should I be taking notes? I thought. *Who am I kidding? I have zero intention of ever touching a cake.*

Before the refrigerator door swung shut, Mom hauled out a huge ball of hard brown dough that looked like a blob of petrified elephant poop and walked toward me with it. Nodding her head, she motioned to the opposite side of the worktable. "Honey, why don't you stand right there? You can watch me for a minute and then jump in whenever you want. It's easy." She grabbed an oversize cookie sheet and began molding the gingersnap dough. Somewhere between the first and second tray, I reached over to grab some dough, Mom and I continued talking, and I started getting the hang of it. The motion was productive, yet pleasantly mind-numbing.

I soon found that there's something simple and satisfying about baking, and I started to understand why Mom liked being out in her kitchen. Scoop, stamp, sugar. Scoop, stamp, sugar. There's an ease and an exactness that comes with the repetition. Put the dough in the oven, bake for ten minutes, and take out perfectly round, delicious gingersnaps every time.

We were nearly finished scooping out the last of the cookie dough when Mom abruptly turned, grabbed a broom, and started sweeping the floor. Our conversation came to a halt, and an awkward silence filled the room. I could tell she was gearing up to say something.

"What is it?" I asked, worried. *Was I doing a bad job?*

With her back to me, Mom took a deep breath. "So, Suz... I was thinking." She stopped sweeping and turned to look directly at me. "Please think about this before you answer." I could see in her face that whatever she was about to ask me meant a lot to her. "What would you think about naming these cookies Susansnaps?"

All the hard stuff I had been through was finally over—the meds, the treatments, the daily doctor's visits. Now I'd get a cookie named after me? I'd spent the last year wanting desperately to blend in. I didn't want to be singled out in any way, let alone this one.

But from the tone of Mom's voice, I knew this was not a casual question. It was calculated, direct, asked with purpose. Mom is a determined person, and there's always a method to her madness. I continued to scoop, stamp, and sugar, lining up the cookies six across and nine deep. I kept my head down, thinking that if I focused on the cookies, I could will away the tears brimming in my eyes. Blinking hard to hold them back, I tried to calm myself. *All right, Susan. It's fine. It's just a cookie.*

Finally, after a few minutes, I answered. "Mom, really? What are you going to say when people ask what a Susansnap is? Or why you picked that name? Who is going to buy these? People who feel sorry for us?" As the questions poured out of me, Mom's face fell. But I kept going. "So we're just going to figure it out as we go? Do you think Aunt Sue would like this?" I should have known better, but I was caught up in my own frustration and confusion.

"Susan, it's just a little cookie that people seem to like. I'm not going to organize a big fund-raiser or run a marathon in your honor. I just want to name this cookie for you and Aunt Sue."

No twenty-three-year-old dreams of a future spent baking gingersnap cookies with her mom. And I certainly never dreamed of having a cookie named after me and Aunt Sue because we both had the same disease. I wanted to say no. I wanted to forget about my cancer. Watching my mom bake Susansnaps every day was not going to make that easy.

But for so long, I had been the sick girl who needed my mom at my side. Maybe this time, she was the one who needed me. So many times, during my worst days of chemo, I had needed her to remind me, "You can do this. You are doing a good job." I had always been able to count on her. Couldn't I finally do something for her in return?

After my initial defensiveness had subsided, I realized that hearing Mom say "Susansnaps" was the sweetest and saddest thing. I started rethinking my reaction. *Susansnaps? I don't know... Susansnaps. Hmm... Maybe it is kind of catchy.*

I was hesitant to put my name on the cookie, but I decided that if that was what Mom really wanted, it would be all right. I have to admit that part of me figured not many people would ever buy the cookies, so it wouldn't really matter. I'm not sure why I questioned Mom about whether Aunt Sue would like the idea. I already knew the answer. Based on everything I knew about her, I'm sure that Aunt Sue would have been somewhere between laughing at Mom's absurd garage business and being her biggest supporter.

Dear Sue,

The first time I worked the dinner shift at Carver's, I worked with you. Remember how nervous I was? It wasn't the twenty-stool counter the two of us would be waitressing or taking customers' orders off the burger menu that scared me; it was the thought of potentially messing up in front of the huge Friday-night crowd—and in front of you. "Laura, you'll be fine. It's no big deal," you said, cool and unruffled. "Besides, it's just hamburgers and pie. It's not life-threatening." Those words stuck with me all night, and I ended up having a great time. We whirled around the restaurant, serving burgers and refilling drinks. We sliced and served our share of Mother and Dad's famous banana-nut cake that night too.

I never would have imagined that thirty-five years later, I'd be baking that same cake for dozens of customers in a stand-alone building next to my house in Atlanta. You won't believe what happened. I was baking out of the house when I got a big order for twenty-six custom cakes from the kids' orthodontist. He ordered them as thank-you gifts for all the dentists who had referred patients to him. I burned up the mixer baking all those cakes. After I ran out of space, I covered our kitchen table in the house with cooling racks and pans. With that, Ken said, "You can do this, and it's time to get you out of the house."

What I should have done, months before, was get a normal job. After Ken's treatment, we were worried about our *family's finances. I could have gone to an elementary school and applied for a teaching position—that would have been the logical thing to do. But that's not what happened. In the midst of Ken getting treatment, losing his job, and losing his health insurance, and despite the fact that we had kids to put through college, multiple cars in the driveway to maintain, and a household to keep up, Ken was totally supportive of me when I wanted to build out a full-fledged commercial kitchen in our garage and start my own bakery. I laugh now, thinking about how ridiculous it sounds. I'm so lucky that Ken has always loved me and believed in me. He didn't even flinch when I first told him my garage-to-kitchen idea. In fact, he was so enthusiastic that I never stopped long enough to figure out how I'd pull it off before I dove right in.*

Looking back, I realize I really didn't know what I was doing. Of course, I knew how to bake a good pie. Mother passed that skill on to us. I was using a few of her and Dad's recipes from the restaurant too. But in terms of the logistics of running a business? I didn't have a clue. And then I talked Susan into working for me. How was I going to manage having an employee when I was barely making a profit? The truth is, I was desperate to have Susan there, so I could keep an eye on her. She was more fragile than she realized. If I could keep her in my shop, even if it meant scrounging up little jobs for her to complete, I'd do it.

There were so many times in those early days that I felt so scared, and then I would think of you. I'd hear your voice saying, "Laura, you'll be fine." I sure hoped we would.

11

Double-Sided Tape

JANUARY IS SUCH A LETDOWN OF A MONTH. THERE are no parties, no festivities, no merriment, no special foods or treats, and people are low on money after holiday shopping. It's a month of resolutions—get back to the gym, get healthy, get a promotion, get a new job, save up for school or vacation or a house. I usually look forward to the new year, but that year I found it hard to. Coming out of treatment played tricks on me. I had a lot to sort through, to figure out what I wanted to do next, but I wasn't sure where I fit in anymore. I didn't want to talk about my cancer, chemo, or radiation. I was ready to leave all that behind. But, somehow, it kept popping up, in conversation and in my own thoughts. And although I was ready to focus on Mom's business, I didn't know what I had to offer.

The first of the year brought a dead halt to Mom's growing business. With those pesky New Year's resolutions under way, suddenly there were no calls, no orders, no cars pulling up the driveway to pick up cakes, pies, cheesecakes, and cookies. Every time I saw a commercial on TV for weight loss, I cringed. Who eats sweets in January?

The loss of income was problematic, of course, but the lack of business was also hard for me, because I was once again facing long days and not much to fill them with. A job with no work? That might sound like a nice deal to some people, but to me, it was frustrating. I started to feel useless again, and I think Mom did too. Together, we started asking, "What comes next? What do we do now?" Mom didn't seem to mind that she had brought me on as an employee and now had nothing for me to do—I think she was just happy she didn't have to give me shots, dole out pills, or sleep on the floor in my room anymore. But I was getting restless.

Around that time, I started to have vivid dreams of Aunt Sue. I had only heard her voice on Mom and Dad's wedding video, and of course I'd seen photos of her, yet she appeared in my dreams, talking to me. But, eerily, rather than being Mom's age, she was in her twenties and looked about my age. I didn't know what to think about that. And then I started having real nightmares that I was stuck in chemo. Dr. Weens would be there, telling me that my treatment hadn't worked, that the cancer hadn't gone away. I wasn't sure I could go through it all again—the chemo, the terrible side effects. I'd be screaming in my nightmares, trapped in this otherworldly treatment. It was terrifying. I'd go out to the shop and try to find something, *anything*, to do, but I couldn't forget those vivid thoughts. The nightmares got worse whenever I had a follow-up doctor's appointment; I'd find myself worrying about what would happen if the cancer wasn't gone. Even an ounce of doubt was hard to shake.

And then there was Randy. He had found a job in Birmingham and was saving up to move to Atlanta and go back to school. There is no guidebook for what he had been through, twenty-one years old with a girlfriend who was recovering from cancer. He didn't know what he could do to help me, and for that matter, neither did I. Randy had been devastated by my diagnosis and tended to imagine the worst. When I would try to make light of something related to my cancer or treatment, he wouldn't find it funny. I worried that it was all too much to ask him to deal with and that I was dragging him down. I knew he meant it when he assured me he didn't feel that way at all and he would do anything for me. For some reason, his reassurances made it easier for me to tell him not to come around too much. Maybe I was pushing him away. I was protective of Randy, but I also didn't want to become some sad, sick, pity case.

One thing I found helpful was when Mom and I got cable in the shop, which sounds like a small thing but was actually life-changing. We plugged in my old eleven-inch TV and were able to enjoy our daily lineup of shows right from the bakery. Between having ongoing conversations about our shows, and then, once business started to pick up again, helping with batches of cookies, putting together shipping boxes, and doodling business card ideas, I had plenty of opportunities to distract myself from my fears.

One morning, we were putzing around in the shop, cleaning and organizing, when I asked Mom, "Did you see the final tally of orders from December?" I held up a clipboard.

It turned out that the tins of gingersnaps, which Mom did end up naming Susansnaps, were our number-one seller. I couldn't believe it. Out of all the delicious desserts my mom baked—cakes, pies, fancy cookies—people liked the simple gingersnaps best. Of course, they were delicious and a quintessential Christmas cookie, but I couldn't help but wonder what exactly made them appealing enough to outsell all our other products.

I thought about the act of gift-giving and how I had received presents while I was sick. People gave me the most random things—a bonsai tree, a bird-watching pamphlet, a coffee-table book called *How to Dress for Success*—probably because they didn't know what to send. Honestly, what do you give a twenty-two-year-old with cancer? And what do you say? That's why, when I gave out Mom's cookies to other patients at my treatments, I kept it simple. "Hang in there." "We're thinking of you." "Hope today goes okay." Finding the right thing to say was especially hard when I was talking to someone who was very sick, since telling them, "Get well soon" was not an option. But thanks to

Mom's bags of delicious cookies, I didn't have to say much at all because the sweets did the talking for me. Maybe that's why the gingersnaps were our bestselling item. They were simple, not over the top—just enough to let someone know you were thinking of them. That was what meant the most to me when I was sick.

One thing that bothered me though, was when people would say things like, "You're going to be fine. It's treatable, right? Oh good, you're fine."

It might have been true that I'd be fine, but at the time, it didn't necessarily feel that way. Nothing about the treatment I was going through was "fine." I was grateful for the drugs and grateful I had excellent medical care, but the treatment process was brutal, and it didn't help to hear people minimize what I was dealing with.

One night, when I was feeling particularly down about not having a job and worried about a relapse, I'd had my fill of hearing things like that from various people. We'd had a nice Sunday dinner with the family, everyone else had left the kitchen, and Mom was doing the dishes. I took a seat at the counter and said, "Mom, if one more person tells me I am going to be fine, I think I'm going to hit them!"

Mom sat down next to me. "Oh, Susan, the things I've heard. Someone stopped me at the grocery store once and said, 'I heard your husband has non-Hodgkin's. Did you know that Jacqueline Kennedy died from that five months after being diagnosed?' Suz, what was I supposed to say back? 'Excuse me, you're blocking the broccoli'?"

Mom and I sat there commiserating about ridiculous things people had said to us until we started laughing so hard we were both in tears. Mom had never shared anything like that with me before. I felt like she was letting me in on a little secret. During that cathartic laugh fest, I realized what really bothered me about people telling me I would be fine was feeling like I had to console them by agreeing with them. "Yes, I'm going to be okay. You're right. It's not that bad. It's not that bad at all. Don't worry. I'm fine!"

Mom reminded me, "It's not your job to make other people feel better about your cancer." I knew she was right, but that was hard to remember sometimes. I wished that, rather than go on and on about how fine I was going to be, someone had just given me a tin of gingersnaps!

.... ❦ ....

We had a new customer, Barbara, who was hooked on Mom's coconut cake and gingersnaps, and she became a frequent visitor to the shop. One afternoon, I saw her pull into the driveway so I headed to the back to get her cake and cookie tins while she chatted with Mom. I leaned into the fridge to pull out the cake, which was resting on its cardboard cake round, but since I have stubby fingers and no nails to speak of, I could not get it off the refrigerator shelf. With no leverage, I chased the three-layer cake as it slid around and around. While I was fumbling with it, trying not to stick my fingers in the frosting, I heard Barbara say, "Laura, have you ever considered taking these cookies to the Mart? The gourmet show? You would do great." My ears perked up. I knew she was talking about the well-known Atlanta International Gift and Home Furnishings Market, which was held a few times a year.

With the cake finally boxed and the tins bagged up, I gave them to Barbara, smiled, and quickly excused myself. Leaving Mom to complete the transaction, I dashed off to the computer to look up the show. We knew about AmericasMart Atlanta, but it had never crossed my mind that Mom and I could sell there. When I clicked on the exhibitor application and saw that it was multiple pages, I figured that there was no point getting my hopes up, or even reading the whole thing, if we couldn't afford to attend. I skipped straight to the information on exhibitor costs.

I learned that it would cost thousands of dollars to enter the show, and for that huge amount of money, we'd only get a ten-square-foot space, two undraped tables, two folding chairs, one wastepaper basket, and preshow vacuuming service. It didn't seem like a great value to me, but I knew that hundreds of successful food vendors and shops attended the show every year. I thought, *Surely, I must be missing something. Why would anyone do this if it didn't work?* Scrolling back to the top of the application, I read the large text that jumped off the screen: "Experience a marketplace unlike any other—one connecting buyers and exhibitors from around the globe… Buyers from all fifty states and more than ninety nations." I knew we had to go to this show if we were serious about our business; to me, it wasn't even a choice.

When I heard the office door open, I spun around in the desk chair. "Mom, come read this. Want to go?" Without much convincing, she agreed to take a look.

The Mart held the gourmet food show four times a year, and the next one happened to be coming up the next week. "It doesn't cost anything just to look," Mom said. "Let's go see what it's about, and then we can consider signing up for the one in September."

It hadn't occurred to me to go on a field trip to research the Mart first, but it was a smart idea. "Sure," I said. "Let's scout out the competition, see what we're up against."

Days later, Mom and I entered the gourmet food floor and instantly found ourselves on sensory overload. The mishmash of odors, from hot sauces and dip mixes to exotic coffees and seafood stews, smelled downright gross. The fluorescent lights were on full blast, illuminating a different eye-catching, colorful display every ten feet, making it hard, at first, to focus. The hum of people shouting over one another was deafening. "Try a sample." "We make the best." "You don't want to pass this up!" Each seller screamed louder than the last, hoping to nab potential customers. The huge room was filled with the urgency of buying, selling, and making deals. While it seemed overwhelming to me, I also felt

excited. But looking back, maybe I was just excited to be out of the
house and doing something new.

As we made our way up and down each aisle, I alternated
between feeling energized and intimidated. Since we didn't
intend to place any orders, we stayed back and observed from
afar, not taking samples or asking questions that could mislead
the vendors. I dissected the elements of each booth—decorations,
displays, even the clothes the vendors were wearing—and took
mental notes; I was enjoying it so much I was almost giddy. Every
few feet I would tap Mom's arm to get her attention. "We can *so*
do this. Did you see that booth two back, on the right? It wasn't
anything special." We walked a little farther, and I commented,
"Simple color schemes make the products pop." Then, "We'll
need an easy way to give out samples." Mom was just as excited
as I was, taking everything in and pointing at the things that
stood out to her.

It felt good to get lost in my ideas and the creative vision
Mom and I were beginning to share. Thinking about the potential
future of our business was suddenly captivating. And it didn't hurt
to see Mom's wheels spinning either. The prospect of exhibiting
at this show was a little intimidating, but I needed to do this. *We*
needed to do this. As we stood back and watched sellers sell, I
realized how much I was longing to latch on to something new,
and I soaked up the energy from everything going on around us.

I saw that most of the companies attending the show had

fully developed product lines with a variety of flavors. Because the products featured here were sold in bulk and shipped all over the country, they had to have a shelf life. Most of our products, including cakes and pies, had to be eaten within a few days after they were baked and couldn't be shipped. Susansnaps were the only product we had that would work for the show. We didn't find any companies selling just one item, and I wondered if we could really bring Susansnaps—our unassuming gingersnaps in a simple red tin—to this type of high-level buying market. I probably should have felt more unsure, but I liked the feeling of being challenged. It would definitely be out of the ordinary to bring just one food item to the Mart and build a business on one product, but that didn't mean we couldn't try it. So, I figured, *Why not?*

As I looked around and took in the booths' elaborate displays, beautiful branding, and creative product packaging, I told myself, *You can do this. It's just cookies. Break this down into small tasks.* Keeping that thought in my mind made the idea we could someday have a booth here seem doable. A ten-by-ten-foot space, a sign, a backdrop, table covers, order forms, and samples of a delicious product. That's all it was.

We continued strolling along and came across an impressive booth of hot chocolate mixes. We stepped inside to browse, and I soon felt the vendor's gaze on us. I tensed up. Had we been outed for just looking around and not placing any orders?

The vendor, an outgoing guy, walked over to us. "Hi! How

are you?" He looked at me and blurted out, "I really like your scarf. You look great."

Caught off guard, I thought, *My* what? *Oh, my head.* I ran my fingers around the knot at the back of my silk scarf and simply said, "Thanks." I had been so lost in the world of gourmet food and imagining a Susansnaps booth that I had managed to forget for a few minutes about the way I looked. Now though, I realized I might look a little funny—and there I'd been thinking that Mom and I were being inconspicuous. I was so used to my scarf that when I'd gotten ready that morning, I'd thought the only weird thing about my outfit was the pair of sensible shoes Mom had asked me to wear.

I eventually found out it could take years before I'd bounce back completely, and my lack of energy was a daily reminder of this. I had willingly agreed to Mom's shoe request that morning because it was better than the alternative—using a wheelchair. She had tricked me into doing that before, when Carey and I went shopping for her homecoming dress, and I wasn't eager to repeat the experience. It was after I'd had a tough round of chemo. I overheard Mom on the phone asking, "Will anyone be using the church's wheelchair tomorrow?"

Coming into the kitchen, I asked, "Mom, what are you doing?"

"Nothing," she said quickly.

"I just heard you," I said. "What's the wheelchair for?"

"Carey said you two are going to the mall to shop for her homecoming dress."

"Yeah. I want to. I think we're going tomorrow." When Mom didn't say anything else, I started to catch on. "Is that what you want a wheelchair for? I don't need that."

"I know you don't."

"Then why are you getting one?"

Mom looked sheepish. "I was just going to drive you girls there and follow along."

"You're going to look silly pushing around an empty wheelchair."

"I'm good with that," she replied. "I'm bringing the wheelchair. Sit, don't sit. I'll have it with me, just in case."

Mom knew the mall could be daunting, and she didn't want Carey or me to be scared if I happened to have an incident, like running out of energy or suddenly becoming dizzy. She'd had an experience like that before, when she'd gone shopping with Aunt Sue, who had an episode that left her out of breath. So the next day, Mom followed behind us with a vacant wheelchair. I can't say Carey and I didn't laugh at her. But by the time we left, I was collapsed in that chair, needing to go home.

Now, I wasn't sure if it was my sneakers or my scarf that had done it, but I was glad we'd caught the attention of that hot chocolate vendor. We got to chatting, and he was actually a really nice guy, telling us the ins and outs of the show and even inviting us to see how he ran his warehouse. He gestured to his impeccably decorated booth and company display, saying, "This might look involved, but there's nothing to it. Besides, it looks like you've done much harder things." It turned out that his mom had some experience with what I had just been through.

Mom and I continued past a few more booths, collecting brochures and catalogs from different vendors as we went. Suddenly, I felt my energy crash, and my feet started dragging. I was done, but we'd been having such a good time I didn't want to say anything. Mom must have sensed it though, because she said, "I think I've seen plenty. How about you?" Back in the car, we spent the whole ride home discussing our ideas, beginning to make a plan of attack.

After our trip to the Mart, Mom and I had more questions than answers, but our creative juices were flowing and ideas were pouring out. We had an extensive to-do list that kept growing. A question as simple as, "How do we ship a case?" would turn into, "How many units fit in a case? Where do we buy packing materials? How much will we charge?"

Hoping to turn our cookie hobby into a real business, Mom and I tried anything and everything we could dream up. We glued together packaging ideas, called local gift stores, snapped product photos for our brochure, and even played tackle football with shipping boxes filled with our cookies, to see how they'd withstand the bumps and falls they'd experience during the shipping process. Our first trial run of sending cookies across the country ended with Mom's friend in California receiving a tin of crumbs. Each week, we'd hack away at one task, project, or question, while still coming up with more ideas.

We didn't sit down and map out a business plan or set goals for what we wanted to accomplish in the next one, two, or five years, but we did sign up and pay for a booth at the September show at the Mart, giving us nine months to get up and going. Then we just started working and plugging away at it. Maybe it wasn't the smartest way to start a business, but it's what we did. It was thrilling and therapeutic to create something from scratch, to start at the bottom and work our way up. And the fact that my mom and I were doing it together made it even better.

We had big ideas for what a cookie company like Susansnaps could become, but we kept our day-to-day operations very simple. We had to, since we didn't have much money to play around with. But even though we tried to keep things simple, we still had difficult challenges to face. We weren't following any textbook, and our only goal at that point was to have a successful show at the Mart. We researched where to buy spices in bulk, how to do custom packaging, and how to build a website. We decided to hire a reputable company in Atlanta to help us build a website. They gave us a new logo, new color scheme, new font, new titles. It was modern and edgy and…nothing at all like Susansnaps. They didn't take us seriously and hadn't listened to what we were envisioning. We ended up paying $6,000 and having no website to show for it. It was money we couldn't afford to lose, and the experience taught us to trust our gut and not let anyone push us around when it came to our creative vision.

For our packaging, we decided to add a label explaining the story behind Susansnaps, describing how Mom had come up with the idea of baking the cookies and naming them after Aunt Sue and me. I was happy to design the label, writing it from Mom's point of view rather than mine, to help her share what she wanted everyone to understand about Susansnaps: these cookies were made from more than just sugar and spice.

One thing had me thinking. It was great that Mom had a recipe for gourmet gingersnaps and that we were selling to a small, but loyal, customer base, but our customer list, which consisted of people around town, a few of my cancer buddies, and my grandparents, didn't exactly amount to a standout track record. I didn't want us to be trying to convince a buyer at the Mart to take a chance on our product with a line like, "My grandparents enjoy these cookies, so they'll do great in your gift store in Virginia!" Somehow that didn't sound very convincing.

So I made a suggestion to Mom. "You know how everyone keeps telling us that they love our cookies with coffee and tea? Maybe we should try to sell to a coffee shop, to get the snaps out to a wider customer base. We could try Starbucks. There's one in the mall."

"Susan, how would we sell there?" Mom said. "Starbucks? They have thousands of stores."

"OK," I said, undeterred. "What about Nordstrom? They have that coffee place near the entrance."

"Sweetie, Nordstrom?" Mom was laughing nervously because she knew I was serious.

"I don't see why not," I said.

Again, I was off to the internet to do research. Clicking through the website of our local Nordstrom store, I announced, "It's called an espresso bar. Here's the number."

"Don't you think we should write to Nordstrom's corporate office?" Mom asked. "Maybe we should see what they think and offer to send samples first."

"No," I responded immediately. "You're good on the phone. Just call the store." It was easy for me to say it was a good idea, but I sure didn't want to make that call.

"Susan, I've never done anything like this before."

"Neither have I, but you're good at talking. I got the number, now you call."

"Oh, thanks," Mom chuckled. "But that doesn't mean that I know how to sell."

"Mom, you're not really 'selling.' You're just going to see if we can get an appointment, so we can show them our packaging and leave a few samples." I quickly added, "What's the worst that can happen? It's just cookies."

Reluctantly, Mom agreed, and as she dialed, I said, "If it's not going well on the phone, hang up. We'll find something else."

The next thing I knew, Mom had landed us a meeting with Nordstrom's buyer for the Southeast region, to be held in less than forty-eight hours. Unfortunately, we weren't quite prepared to meet so soon—we didn't have packaging or pricing yet—so we had to scramble. While I tried repeatedly to get our home printer to produce some decent printouts of our labels, Mom was baking hundreds of gingersnaps. "Susan," she said, "we need fifteen *perfect* cookies."

We bought small, food-safe plastic packets from The Container Store, placed our homemade labels on the front and back of each one with double-sided tape, filled them with three cookies each, wrapped a ribbon around the middle and secured it with glue, and finished by sealing the opening with our foot-press heat-sealing machine. Admiring our quick product mock-up, which actually looked pretty good, Mom asked, "What do you think we should wear?"

"I don't know," I answered, not having given it any thought. "It's a sales meeting, so I guess we should dress up?"

I considered wearing my interview suit, but I had purchased that at a different time for a different purpose, and I couldn't quite face getting it out for this meeting. We could have worn aprons and jeans, as befits a couple of bakers, but we ended up going with all-black business attire. They say you can never be overdressed. Well, we were.

I didn't know about Mom, but I was so nervous walking to the third-floor offices at our local Nordstrom. The woman Mom had spoken to, Sharon, greeted us courteously and invited us to take a seat in her office. For a second, I couldn't believe I was sitting across the desk from a buyer for the elegant Nordstrom department store. I had no idea what I was doing or how this would go, but at least we were having a meeting. Mom dove in and started describing how our unique product would be a great fit and a delicious choice for their customers, just as we had practiced back home. I didn't see what the buyer's initial reaction was, because I wasn't looking at her. I was watching Mom, feeling somewhere between awestruck and dumbfounded. She sounded like she had been selling our cookies to big-name customers for years. When I heard her mention our packaging options, I realized it was my turn to jump in. I pulled our prototypes out of my bag and placed them on the desk, announcing, "Three cookies per unit, and twenty-four units to a case."

Mom kept talking, explaining the story of Susansnaps while I stared at the samples I had just laid out. *Oh no*, I thought. *These looked better at home.*

The woman was pleasant and nodded as Mom spoke, but she seemed preoccupied with finding something in her desk drawer. Then, somewhat abruptly, she said, "I like your packaging and what you do, and I think this could be a good fit for us." We had been in her office for less than seven minutes.

I don't know what else I thought she'd ask us, but it didn't seem like a good sign that the conversation was already over. She took the samples, the price list we had come up with, and a write-up on our business. She stood up and thanked us for stopping by. Trying to gauge her thoughts, I noticed she was smiling as she added, "We'll look forward to trying the gingersnaps. I have to submit this to corporate before I can get back to you. I'll let you know."

We walked about twenty-five feet from her office, then I couldn't stay quiet any longer. "I think we did well. Mom, you were good."

"I think she liked it," Mom said. "We'll see. I hope she at least considers us for this store."

I was dreaming bigger than that. "Mom, if she chooses us for this store, then why not give us a try in all five stores in her region?"

A couple of days passed with no word from Sharon. We hadn't told anyone we were meeting with Nordstrom, so if she turned us down, no one would know the difference. But three days after our meeting, an email landed in our inbox while I was on the office computer. I gasped and turned around to call for Mom, but she was upstairs in the kitchen. The floor between the shop and the office was thick concrete, so she couldn't hear me. I grabbed the broom that I kept next to the computer and tapped the ceiling as hard as I could with the handle—our signal for "come here."

The door opened and I spun around. "Mom! We got an

email from Nordstrom." I couldn't tell her what it said; she had to see it with her own eyes. Not one store. Not five stores. *One hundred ten stores.* We were approved to sell to all of Nordstrom's espresso bars throughout the country.

Our crazy idea had paid off. Mom and I were ecstatic. We had tried and tried, and that time, it worked. That was our first major sale. The name recognition alone made us happy. Then the orders started coming in. Each store ordered separately, and because the coffee bars are small, without much retail space, they could only take two cases at a time. That added up to just 144 cookies per order. But this was huge—the exposure put us on the map!

Dear Sue,

Carey and Susan thought it was nutty of me to make them take a wheelchair on their shopping trip when Susan was sick. I got that. But I couldn't forget what happened to you decades ago on our own shopping trip.

You'd recently been released from the hospital, following an emergency tracheotomy surgery. Your cancer had advanced to the point where your throat had closed, and you had spent some time in the ICU. You wanted me to go shopping with you at Pier 1. I would have gone anywhere with you, but that doesn't mean I wasn't nervous. You weren't well enough to drive, so I did. We went to check out candles, incense, beaded wall dividers, and all the latest bohemian trends. While there, you started coughing uncontrollably, and your face turned red, as you could not catch your breath. Terrified you would stop breathing, I looked around, wondering if I'd need to call for help again. You calmly went to a quiet spot in the store and pulled the center tube out of your neck in order to clear your air passage. You carried on like it was no big deal. I held my breath until I knew you were okay. How did you do that? You made it seem normal.

When I suggested that we should go home, you said, "No, I'm fine. Besides, I'm not done shopping yet." So, Sue, I couldn't let the girls go without the wheelchair, just in case something happened. Or maybe I couldn't let them go without me.

Changing the subject, I have to tell you: Susan tricked me into making our first corporate call for Susansnaps. After she handed me the phone number, I thought, I have to call? Why me? *It probably wouldn't surprise you that Susan continued,* "Mom, you're good at talking." *Well, she sort of had me there. I'm not sure if I'm any good at it, but I've certainly done my share. At the time, I remember thinking that I wasn't going to say no to Susan—just like I couldn't say no to going to Pier 1 with you. Next thing I knew, I was talking to a buyer for an elegant department store's coffee café. I couldn't really believe what I was doing, talking about a cookie with your and Susan's shared name.*

12

You Want Me to Do What?

NOT LONG AFTER WE LANDED THE NORDSTROM SALE, Mom and I decided to donate some cookie gifts to a benefit for cancer research. We figured it would be a small way for us to give back and, perhaps, attract a few new customers in the process. The American Cancer Society's Hope Fashion Show, held annually in Atlanta, was coming up soon. We'd learned about this lovely fundraiser the year before, when a friend of Mom's invited us to attend, to get out of the house for a few hours during Dad's chemo. Held at the Ritz-Carlton, it was a delightful event featuring a luncheon, drinks, merriment, raffles, a guest speaker, and a fashion show with models who had survived cancer. Looking for ways to grow our business, I thought, *This will be great. There will be five hundred of Atlanta's fanciest ladies packed in one room. A captive audience.* I said to Mom, "We know the snaps are good. Once the attendees take a bite, hopefully they'll want more." We were elated at the thought of Susansnaps making their grand gala debut.

One day, as the event approached, Mom and I had baked a few batches of cookies and shipped some orders, which was a full day's work for me, as I still became exhausted after three or four hours on my feet. After we'd finished up for the afternoon, I headed into the house to turn on the TV, while Mom went to the office to check voicemail. I was lying on the couch next to Carey, waiting for *Oprah* to come on at four o'clock, just like we did every day. Mom came around the corner and plopped down in the chair beside us with a sigh.

"Mom, what's wrong?" I asked.

"Not a thing," she replied. "We heard back from the organizer of the fashion show, and they're thrilled to have our donation. She wanted to know if we could provide fifty gift boxes to use as part of the centerpieces."

"That's great! But you seem kind of upset. Are you sure there's nothing wrong?"

"No. The woman I spoke to was really nice." Despite her cheerful words, it was obvious that something was going on. She hadn't even glanced at the TV and sat there fidgeting, twirling her wedding ring around and around. Then she said, "The coordinators read about you, sweetie. On the back of the box we left them. They thought it would be nice to have you model. She asked if you would."

My breath caught in my throat. "You want me to do *what*?" I asked, hoping I hadn't heard her clearly. I thought back to last year's fashion show. I had just about clapped my hands off during the standing ovation at the end, cheering for the survivors striding up and down, showing off a variety of outfits and styles.

"They want you to be one of the models," Mom repeated.

"Mom, are you serious right now? No. I'm not doing that. Did you already tell them I would? What did you say?"

"I would never answer for you. I told her I would call her back after I'd checked with you."

I felt my face flush. My thoughts started to race. *They want me to be a cancer-survivor model? To sashay along an airport-length runway in the middle of a ballroom with hundreds of people staring at me? Has Mom lost her mind? No way. Absolutely not. I don't want to be paraded around so people can feel sorry for me.*

I knew why they wanted me on that runway; I'd done fund-raising events before. A tagline like "Young girl just out of treatment takes the runway" sells, and the women who organized this event were in the business of bringing in big bucks for life-saving research. I was all for that, and it was flattering that they thought I could help. But it was *too soon.*

I could still barely get my head around being sick in the first place, and now they wanted me to step out as a cancer survivor? I'd spent the last year wanting to be seen and treated simply as Susan, who had just happened to get sick. I didn't want to be different, singled out, or treated specially in any way. How could I step on a runway and publicly announce, *Look at me—the cancer girl!* when I couldn't even say it to myself?

Part of me felt guilty for getting upset. I was lucky enough to get cancer during a time when treatment existed that could cure me. Aunt Sue was diagnosed in the sixties, before men had even landed on the moon. I was far more fortunate, and I was acutely aware of that, but that didn't mean any of this had been easy.

Mom was waiting patiently for my response. Reluctantly, I said, "Mom, really? I don't think so."

"You don't have to. I'll call back and thank them and let them know that you will not be able to help this time."

Did she have to use those words? She knew I would hear, *You* won't *help, and you're letting people down.* Sometime between hanging up the phone with the event coordinator and coming to ask me about being a model, Mom had already decided this was a great idea. That's classic Mom—once she makes up her mind, there's no turning back. Why didn't she just ask me to do this for her? Realizing that she really wanted me to be a model, I started to reconsider.

I couldn't tell her no. I had depended on her, and the last eleven months had been exhausting for both of us. So, although I wasn't happy about it, I told her I would join the other survivors as a model at the event.

A few weeks later, as we drove to the fashion show, I

started yawning, my way of settling my nerves. It wasn't working. All I could think was, *What's going to happen when I step on that runway? Why did I agree to do this?* As we pulled up to the elegant entrance of the Ritz-Carlton, my palms were pooling with sweat. Anxiously, I asked, "Mom, can you please move around the valet line and self-park?" I wasn't sure if it was motion sickness or a bad case of the jitters, but I needed to stop and sit still for a moment. Looking down and fiddling with my fingers, I tried to convince myself it would be okay. *You agreed to do this. You won't disappoint anyone. It'll be over soon.*

Exuding enough confidence for both of us, Mom led the way to the check-in table in the hotel lobby. As the woman manning the table searched for our names and a welcome packet, Mom leaned forward and said quietly, "My daughter, Susan, is one of your models."

The woman smiled and said, "We're so happy to have you. The other survivors are down the hall to the right. We've provided a complimentary hair stylist and makeup artist for your special day."

Instantly self-conscious, I reached to tuck my long blond hair behind my ears, out of habit, but instead my fingers ran along the short brown curls that had started to grow back since my treatments had ended. I'd been poked, prodded, and pulled so much out of necessity by the medical community that the thought of having my hair and makeup done was too much. I whispered in Mom's ear, "I don't think I can have anyone touch me."

Mom looked at me and patted my arm. She turned to the woman and bailed me out, saying, "Thank you, that's very thoughtful, but I think we're all set. What time would you like us in the dressing room?"

I was ready to do this thing, but she told us the fashion show wasn't going to begin for an hour and a half. Sensing that I was uneasy, Mom said, "Let's go see what's in the silent auction. Maybe we'll bid on something?"

We perused the items for the silent auction, wandering around among women dressed to the nines—some in classy pantsuits, others in floral dresses with coordinating hats, a few in sequined casino wear. It was almost impossible not to get caught up in the hubbub. The air filled with chatter and gaiety as the ladies hugged one another, catching up with old friends. Waiters clad in bow ties and tuxes popped up with silver trays, asking, "Pink punch? White wine or champagne?" Some poor volunteer tried to make an announcement over the loudspeaker, but her voice was totally lost in the hullabaloo. The lobby began to spin. *Focus, Susan. Focus.*

Just before my thoughts began to race out of control, Mom winked at me and said quietly, "Look over there."

"Where?" I asked. "Which way?"

Mom started pivoting on one foot, trying to look nonchalant. "Just a minute. Don't look yet."

I didn't know what I was about to see, but I was already

amused by Mom's silly antics. "What is it?" I asked, not daring to look around.

Standing directly in front of me now, Mom said, "You'll see! Look over my left shoulder. You can't miss it."

There, in clear view, was Scarlett O'Hara herself. A woman standing near one of the silent-auction tables was wearing a gown and a hat that looked like they had come straight from the opening scene of *Gone with the Wind*.

"Wow, that's fancy all right!" I said. "I guess we missed the memo?"

Trying not to laugh, Mom said, "I hope she bought two seats. Her hat is huge!"

Thank goodness for that magnificent hat. It kindly provided my mom and me with a moment of entertainment that helped me keep my nerves in check. A few minutes later, Mom moved toward a wall and ran her finger down the seam of the wallpaper. "I couldn't tell if this was paint or wallpaper," she said. "What do you think of it?"

"The paper or the color? I like wallpaper."

As Mom verbally redecorated the lobby, I felt at ease. We share this odd but wonderful ability to get lost in creative visions, reveling in colors, patterns, and designs. It's a unique way for us to escape, and Mom was using it to distract me. Hanging on her every word as she transformed the space around us, I felt like we were the only two people in the room. Then I saw her glance at her watch, and my heart skipped a beat. "I think it's time we head back," she said.

With each step we took down the hallway toward the stage, my apprehension grew. My heart began pounding again, my palms sweating. I tried to calm myself down: *You can do this.* But as soon as I saw the dressing room, I wasn't so sure. Mom stopped at the doorway, like a proud mother dropping off her kindergartener for the first day of school, but I walked right past the door, so that she had to walk briskly to catch up to me.

Something was throwing me off. It wasn't nerves about walking down the runway or wearing a silly outfit—it was something else. I'd gotten good at moving through life as a patient, but that was over now. I didn't know where I fit in anymore. Many of the women at the event were breast cancer survivors; I was a bit of an oddball having Hodgkin's. The vast majority of them were also decades older than me. In many ways, my life was so different from theirs. I had never had a career, I wasn't married, and I lived at my parents' house, in my childhood bedroom. I didn't even have a car. My life had not gone the way I planned. My claim to fame was that I had sat in a recliner, watched the clouds go by, been brought to the brink of death and back, and come out the other side, all before I turned twenty-three. Being at the fashion show made me notice this in a way I hadn't before. And I felt broken.

Being there, out in public, I felt like my fragile state was terribly exposed. As I had grown weaker, Mom had become stronger for me. She'd been my warrior, my shield, my advocate. I hadn't realized how much I counted on her. We had done all of this together. But now, I was going to have to go out on that stage alone.

I moved to the end of the hallway to find some privacy, trying to pull myself together and feeling frustrated that I was cracking in public. Calmly, Mom came up behind me and asked, "What is it, honey?"

My heart sank. This was supposed to be Mom's day. I didn't want her to think I was mad at her for bringing me here. I knew I could do this. It all just seemed to be happening so fast. One minute I had been an ordinary college student, the next I was undergoing treatment for cancer, and now I was at an over-the-top gala about to step onto a runway. First a girl, then a sick girl, now a survivor?

I closed my eyes for a second, trying to block out my overwhelming feelings. I turned to Mom but couldn't look her in the eye, knowing that if I did, the tears would start flowing and probably not stop. "Do any of these people know why they're here?" I asked. I paused to gather my thoughts, then continued in a flurry. "There are patients right now, right this minute, who are horribly sick."

"Honey, I know," Mom said. "You're right—there are. You have every right to be upset. I know this looks like one big party, but they're trying to help."

She was right, of course. But it was hard to see past the fancy decorations and expensive clothes. All that was going through my head were pictures, images, faces of patients we'd met during my treatment. I was aching for all those people, and for the first time, I really understood that *I had been one of those people...* But I wasn't anymore. For months, I'd been harboring this feeling of survivor's guilt, and it was magnified that day. I asked myself, *Why me?* Not, *Why did I get cancer?* But, *Why did I survive?* Some of my chemo and radiation buddies weren't going to make it. But, for some reason, I had. Aunt Sue had died, and twenty-seven years later, I had lived. Not a day went by that I didn't think about that.

Trembling from emotional overload, I said, "This isn't easy."

Mom grasped my hand tightly and simply said, "I know."

Finally, I was able to say the words that had been swirling around inside me. "Mom, I will never be the same." That's what was nagging at me, making me feel uncomfortable and nervous. I finally had to admit my cancer had changed me forever.

Before Mom could say anything else, a volunteer made her way over to us. Flinging her arms around me, she said, "Oh dear! Are you nervous? You'll be a great model." Still squeezing me, she looked at Mom, adding, "We're going to take good care of her. Feel free to go ahead and take your seat." Talk about bad timing.

My tears stopped as I tried to pull away from her awkward side-armpit embrace. With a coolness and poise I knew only came from masking her own fears, Mom said pointedly, "Susan's fine. We're okay. I'm not ready to go to my seat quite yet, but thank you." I think the volunteer got the hint, because she backed away.

With that, I heard the chime of the xylophone calling the last of the guests into the ballroom. Mom turned to me and said, "You don't have to do this."

"No, I want to," I said. "I'm sorry. I didn't know until we got here that this was going to be so hard."

With tears in her eyes, Mom said, "I'm proud of you."

"I know," I said, looking down at the carpeted floor.

She grabbed both my hands. "Look at me. I'm proud of you."

"Mom, it's okay. You can take your seat." Now was not the time for this. Why hadn't we talked about all this sooner?

"There are hundreds of people in that room, and I want you to know that I'm the luckiest one." Her voice broke. "You let me be there for you. I watched your bravery for months. I'm in awe of how you've handled yourself."

"Mom, it's okay. We're fine. I'll see you in a bit."

Just as my role as a patient had ended, so had Mom's as my caretaker. I had been her sole focus over the past year. Being at the charity event was an outward acknowledgment of the fact that we were moving on. My apprehension dissolved as I realized I was only doing this for one person, and she was right in front of me. I didn't care about anyone else in that room but my mom.

As I stood in the dressing room with the other models, I

stayed off to the side, not wanting to be seen. I planned to walk down the runway and back and then go straight to the car to head home. As I listened to the conversations and stories the women around me were sharing, I heard them comparing their experiences. I caught myself absentmindedly running my fingers across the scar on my neck. A few months ago, I was spending my Fridays hooked up to IVs, and now, somehow, I was a survivor. A survivor of what? I'd just done what was in front of me, whatever the doctors and nurses told me to do. I hadn't done anything special. There was no one reason why I had survived and the next person hadn't. As I looked around the room and saw so many vivacious women, I realized I was one of the lucky ones.

At last, I changed into the outlandish attire that had been selected for me: a patterned shirt with excessive ruffles, high-waisted black denim mom jeans, and a matching corseted jacket trimmed in leather and lace, accessorized with a black belt with hammered silver filigree to complete the look. It was definitely not my style, but by then, I didn't care. Without even glancing in the mirror, I took my place in line.

We'd been given a seating chart, so I knew Mom's table was at the end of the runway, on the left. As I waited behind the black curtain, I planned my runway strategy, deciding to look at Mom once, smile, then look away and turn back down the runway.

It was chaotic backstage, and I tried to stay out of the way of professional models changing in and out of the newest spring collections and stylists adding finishing touches. Quietly, I watched the line ahead of me dwindle to nine women, then eight, then seven. Any last reservations that I might have had were drowned out by the blaring, upbeat music, the emcee shouting each model's name and backstory, and the applause from the enthusiastic crowd. Then, suddenly, I was up next. With a quick look up to the heavens and a slight smile to myself, I stepped out onto the runway.

For a few seconds, all I could see were bright lights. Before I took even one step forward, I focused on finding Mom. She was beaming with pride, and her giant smile was reassuring. My eyes met hers for a split second. *I've got this, Mom.* Taking a deep breath and looking straight forward, I threw my shoulders back and stood taller. My feet began to glide down the platform. *Look at me. Here I go.*

Over the roar of the crowd, I heard the emcee announce, "Twenty-three years old…four months out of treatment…her Aunt Sue…her dad…cookie company…Susansnaps on your tables…"

I felt my insecurities melt away. The crowd was clapping, and there were audible gasps, laughs, and cheers. *That's me!* By the time I'd made it back up the runway, I felt amazing. Being a survivor may not define who I am, but it is definitely a part of me. Remaining on the stage with the others to receive a standing ovation, I looked out at Mom again. I shrugged my shoulders, and we both laughed. *We did it.*

I'm not sure if it was our cookies on the table, my introduction on the runway, or perhaps the ridiculous outfit I was modeling, but something about me caught the attention of a journalist who had attended the fashion show. She called and made arrangements with Mom to visit our shop, and less than twenty-four hours later, Jennifer, a journalist from the *Atlanta Journal-Constitution*, the city's leading newspaper, was on her way to our garage bakery for an interview.

Jennifer was nice, but since it was an informal visit, it was hard to decipher what were interview questions and what was just her own personal intrigue. I did find it curious that Mom had baked a variety of cakes and pies for her to sample, but she didn't take a single bite. Instead, we got into talking about the gingersnaps, Aunt Sue, Mom and I working together, and even my treatment. She jotted down a few lines on her spiral notepad. It meant a lot to us that Jennifer had taken the time to come meet us and see our shop, and she seemed pleased when she left, saying, "I got what I need." I thought we'd done a nice job, but there was no way to know.

On Sunday morning, I woke up to Mom whispering, "Susan, are you awake? Want to ride with me to get a newspaper?"

"Yeah, I'll meet you outside," I said.

I was scrounging through Mom's purse for quarters as we pulled into the gas station. "How many copies should we buy?"

"Get one, and let's see if they put anything in," said Mom.

What did she mean, *put anything in*? Jennifer had left us certain that she'd gotten what she needed to write an article.

I popped a couple of quarters into the newspaper dispenser and grabbed the top copy. Sitting in the parking lot, I pulled apart the paper and handed Mom a few sections. I quickly flipped through mine. "I don't see anything. Where's the food section?"

"Hold on a minute. Maybe there's a review or small business section in the back."

Almost before Mom could finish her sentence, I began laughing. "Mom!"

"What?"

I held the newspaper away from her so she couldn't see. "We're in the paper!"

"Okay. Well, let me see!"

"No. I mean, we—*you and I*—are in the newspaper."

I turned the living section toward Mom, unveiling a full-color photo of the two of us baking cookies, beneath a headline that read, "Sweet and Powerful."

As Mom grabbed the paper to get a closer look, I exclaimed, "We're the feature story! Turn the page, it keeps going."

She flipped the page. "Oh no. There's another picture of us!"

I read the article over Mom's shoulder, zeroing in on the sentence that read, "Cookies are weapons in their war against family's illnesses." This exposure was unbelievable, and I was in shock. *Is that me? Is that what I look like now?* It was weird seeing myself in print. I'd been sure Jennifer was going to profile Mom's baking, and she'd at least mention her award-winning banana-nut cake or her decadent chocolate chip cheesecake. But apparently, she had found the reason why we bake our gingersnaps and how we started working together more interesting.

What a week. And to think, I had been worried about five hundred women staring at me at a charity event. Now we were featured in the Sunday paper. Looking out my window as we drove home, I couldn't help but notice a newspaper with our article in it sat on each and every driveway. Knowing that those papers would soon be read, I wondered out loud, "Mom, do you think we'll get any response?"

Dear Sue,

You had a beautiful voice and loved singing so much. Even though you would get nervous and splurge on pricey Mitchum antiperspirant, your onstage performance with your high school choral group meant so much to you that it was worth it. But modeling on a stage would have been unthinkable for you. Of course, there weren't any elaborate fund-raising events back then, so a fashion show like the one Susan participated in wouldn't even have been a possibility. But besides that, we couldn't even make it across my bedroom in Mother's high heels, trying to mimic the beauty queens of the day, without our ankles wobbling. Most of all, you never wanted anyone making a fuss over you. The fewer people who knew about your disease the better. And your humility made me love you all the more.

So why did it mean so much to me to see Susan on that stage? Good question. When I cracked open the door to the expansive ballroom and saw fifty tables set with ten places each, I nearly panicked. I thought, What in the world have I done to her? *I know, I should have thought it through more carefully before I convinced her to model at the gala. But I couldn't help myself. I knew that Susan would remind those women that cancer can happen to anyone. When Susan stepped out from behind the curtain, the ballroom exploded with deafening applause. She didn't even flinch. I was amazed by her grace and self-confidence. She didn't quite look like her old self yet, but there was a radiance in her face I hadn't seen before. I was watching Susan and seeing some part of you. I know that Susan did this for me…and maybe she stepped out there for you too.*

13

This Little Cookie
Went to Market

NOTHING EVER GOES QUITE THE WAY WE EXPECT, AND that article in the paper was no exception. If we had expected the phone to start ringing off the hook, we would have been wrong. We did get a few calls from people wanting to buy gingersnaps and share stories about their own friends or family undergoing cancer treatment. Those comments meant a great deal to us, but they were hardly a deluge of business.

We got eight orders from that article. It wasn't much, but we were happy. As far as we were concerned, there were eight new people who were going to share the cookies with at least eight more people. Then we'd have sixteen customers.

The article also brought about an unexpected visit from our local NBC affiliate. It was just a short spot, and we had no idea what we were doing on TV (that's another story), but it resulted in the owner of Sydney's Spices, a local store, offering us a free, one-year supply of spices for our gingersnaps.

Mom and I were delighted. We took this feedback as encouragement to keep going. We weren't getting more than a few orders a week, but at least it was a start.

We took the opportunity to think bigger. I wondered, *If that* Atlanta Journal-Constitution *journalist was interested, who else might be?* I thought if I could get us into another newspaper, that would mean a handful more people who'd know about us. Building our business one customer at a time was fine with us. After our article ran in the *AJC*, I contacted our three neighborhood newspapers. And we continued to prepare for the show at the Mart. As Mom sewed together three-inch strips of fabric, alternating black and white, for our tablecloths and jigsawed wood to make display stands, I tried my hand at writing about our mother-daughter business. I worked on a little blurb about our home-based operation that I hoped would spark the curiosity of buyers in our booth. We naturally divided tasks. Mom was doing her part, and I was pitching in too.

I learned at an early age that a job half-done is a job not done at all. In our family, Saturday mornings meant chores. One Saturday, when I was seven, I was assigned to dusting. I grabbed a rag and ran to the living room so I could be the first one to call out, "Mom, I'm all done."

We had to pass inspection. As Mom came around the

corner, she said, "You finished very quickly. Are you sure you want me to look?"

I had swirled the rag around and collected some dust, so I said, "Yes, I'm ready."

As Mom lifted the candleholders from the end table, I cringed.

Swiping the table with her fingertips, she said, "Susan, I thought you said you were done. Is this your best?"

"No," I said, knowing I hadn't followed through. "I can fix it."

But it was too late. Mom took the rag and said, "You had your chance. You should have done it right the first time."

I felt awful as I watched her take the items off the table and show me how to do a thorough job. As she completed my task, she shared some wisdom. "You know, Susan, when you do a job partway, it's like you never did it at all." I didn't like being called out for not trying my hardest, and I decided right then it would never happen again.

So when it came to exhibiting at the Mart, I was all in. I had "learned to dust," and that lesson applied to this too. This was it. We'd spent nine months preparing, and now, it was showtime—not for me or for Mom, but for our gingersnaps. We didn't know how the show would go or if our idea would work, but we were about to find out.

When the day to set up our booth arrived, I went out to the shop early and began counting how many containers we had to pack in Mom's car. We'd filled twelve clear plastic storage bins with our time, creativity, and marketing skills. Looking at this stack that we'd poured our hearts and souls into, I was amazed at the amount of work we had done to turn one cookie into a company. Mom and I were finally just an hour away from taking our menagerie of signs, backdrops, lights, and product samples, and transforming them for the next three days into a Susansnaps display and sales center.

As I slid our toolbox and collapsible stools into the car, Mom came up behind me and asked, "Are we going to make it all fit?"

"I'm not sure," I said, "but it's fine. We can always come back for more or just take the rest tomorrow." Mom went around to the trunk and started jimmying and juggling the containers, trying to create more open space. It definitely looked like we weren't going to be able to fit everything.

So we hadn't quite thought this part through. When we created our display, we never factored in how we were going to get it to the show. I could tell Mom was stressing out. She seemed to be regarding the overloaded car as some kind of personal failure, but the packing process was simply something we had overlooked.

Seeing that she was hell-bent on not leaving anything behind, I said, "All right, Mom. I can always hold something."

"Great," she said. "I can fit more in if you move your seat up."

I jumped into the front passenger seat and scooted forward, calling, "Is this good?"

"No, pull up as far as you can."

I started laughing. "If I go any farther, I'll be on the hood of the car!"

As I somehow yanked the seat forward a teensy bit more, Mom was able to wedge in another container, and she declared, "We're in!" Plopping the last bucket into my lap, Mom instructed, "Don't move. I'll get the rest."

"The rest?" I was beginning to feel like one of those clowns packed into a miniature car at the circus.

After a minute, Mom came back and said, "Watch your left arm." As I looked over my shoulder, six eight-foot PVC pipes and four wooden risers slid past my head, resting between the two front seats. Slamming the trunk shut, Mom shouted, "That's it!"

Usually, I don't mind Atlanta's skyscrapers, traffic, and one-way streets, but I have to admit that circling the Mart's expansive buildings, which cover four city blocks and house seven million square feet of exhibition space, was intimidating. As we moved toward the loading dock, I realized how silly our little car looked next to the big vans and trucks with professionally printed company names and logos that were steering around us. For months, our goal had been to do everything we could to get ready for the show. Now, we didn't just want to be there; we wanted to do well. I felt energized by the challenge. Looking out the window, I saw license plates from Tennessee, Ohio, Utah, and

Arizona. People were all over the streets and sidewalks, unloading massive trucks and taking dollies, forklifts, and pallets in and out of the convention center. Meanwhile, we were in a small black Volvo. We had one cookie to sell. Clearly, we were going to be the underdog, and I felt a competitive edge coming back to me, something I hadn't noticed just working in the shop.

Mom and I had invested the better part of our holiday profits into the trade show entrance fee and preparations. But even more than that, we had poured our emotions, love, and passion into this cookie. Our gingersnaps weren't simply flour, sugar, and spices. They had been an outlet for us, a therapeutic release, for months. As we got stronger, our business did too. It had been exhilarating to work and focus on creating, dreaming, and doing—to figure out, on our own, each step of the process. And together, we had.

If we'd been going to the Mart to sell something generic, like chocolate chip cookies, then maybe I wouldn't have felt like so much was at stake. The mere fact that we called our cookies Susansnaps represented an unspoken commitment we'd both made to get this right, to not fail, to give it our all. It represented Aunt Sue's name, my name, and an idea Mom and I shared. I hadn't realized until that moment just how much of a healing process building Susansnaps had been.

As we pulled up to the loading dock, I finally said out loud what I suspect we both had been thinking. "There's no turning back now."

A dock worker tapped on Mom's window. As she rolled it down, he shouted, "Ma'am, you got a dock pass?"

Handing over our document, Mom proudly announced, "Yes, we are here for the gourmet food show."

The worker said, "All right, ma'am. We'll getcha taken care of." As he directed us closer, Mom cautiously steered the car between two semis.

"We didn't pay for extra help," I reminded her.

Mom nodded and said, "Suz, get out. Grab something. We can do it ourselves."

With my arms full of boxes, I heard Mom call out, "Thank you. We've got it." We might have thought we were doing a great job of blending in, but the mere size of our car outed us as newbies. A forklift pulled up next to our car, and the operator called, "Mmm! Sure smells good." Staring at our humble pile of boxes among the towering pallets being unloaded from other vendors' trucks, he started teasing Mom. "Lady, is this all you got? If that's it, give me your booth number, and I'll lead the way."

In no time flat, we entered the vast floor dedicated to gourmet food exhibits. As we made our way through the industrial superstructure, which had been divided into row after row of selling stalls, I couldn't help but think how different walking the aisles felt today, compared to when we'd visited nine months ago. It wasn't the fact that we were vendors now that made it different—it was me. I felt different. My follow-up appointments were growing farther apart. Now, when I woke up in the morning, nothing ached. I had no pain, no sickness, no nausea. Each day, I felt a bit more like my old self.

We arrived at our assigned sales space and took in its cold concrete floor, sad gauzy drapes, and trash can. A flimsy, dangling sign displayed our booth number; I felt like it was screaming at us, *All this for the bargain price of $3,200!* As Mom thanked the forklift operator for his help, I stared at our pitiful booth. Allowing myself only a split second of buyer's remorse, I asked, "Where should we start?"

"Let's get the backdrop up first," Mom said. "These beige walls are depressing." She pulled out our black-and-white polka-dot fabric and eyed our eight-foot PVC frame. "Grab a handful of safety pins."

Before I could attempt to find a ladder, Mom was already balancing one foot on an unstable stool, calling out, "Hand me one." When she had the backdrop halfway up, she asked, "How does it look?"

With one hand holding pins and the other steadying Mom's foot on the stool, trying to prevent her from falling off, I answered, "I don't know. I can't tell from here."

"I'm fine here. Step back and look."

Moving back and glancing up, I exclaimed, "Ooh, I like it!" As Mom finished hanging the backdrop, I was beginning to feel a sense of accomplishment.

Working together, Mom and I popped up folding tables and built risers with cinder blocks, bricks, and wooden planks. Next, we assembled our signs by suspending oversize posters from PVC pipes that we'd fastened to the tables with C-clamps and wooden holders. Finally, unpacking the multitude of bakery bags, gift boxes, and tins we'd designed, we began organizing and setting up our displays of gingersnaps. We stepped around and over each other, paying close attention to every detail and diligently completing the look we'd spent all spring and summer planning. Somehow, our carefully crafted setup was starting to look pretty impressive.

Finally, Mom and I allowed ourselves to step back together and admire our efforts. After six hours and one run to Home Depot for black carpeting, I liked what I saw. The booth looked good—whimsical yet professional. Seeing Mom's handsewn tablecloths and backdrop in coordinating black-and-white fabrics, my logo designs blown up on giant signs, glistening glass jars filled with freshly baked gingersnaps, and more than twenty different packaging options lined up in perfect rows, I was astonished by what we had accomplished. We had certainly put our creativity to the test in stretching our tiny budget. We high-fived, and Mom said, "I think we can call it a day."

We arrived early the next morning, before the show got too chaotic. I flipped on the spotlights and filled cookie jars with samples while Mom organized the "office," which consisted of two clipboards, our business cards, calculators, a cash box, and some odd-looking paper. Quizzically, I inquired, "Mom, what is that?"

Holding up a sheet of what looked like midnight-blue tissue paper, she said, "This? It's carbon paper."

"What are you going to use that for?"

"How else would you propose we make a copy of an order?"

I laughed. "Mom, where'd you buy that?"

"Your dad and I, everyone, used this in college."

"So you saved this from the seventies?" We both cracked up.

"No, I bought it. Thank you very much."

As nutty as this was, it wouldn't be a laughing matter if I didn't know how to use it; I didn't want to be caught fumbling with it in front of a customer. Wanting a trial run, I reached over to take the paper. Mom pulled it away. "Be careful," she warned. "You can only touch the outside corners or permanent ink will get all over you."

The closer it got to nine o'clock, when the floor would officially open for business, the more my uncertainty grew. I tried to stay calm, but it was nearly impossible as activity on the floor picked up and the noise level rose. I focused on what I would say to potential customers to get them interested in our product, hoping we wouldn't have too many lookie-loos and just sample takers.

Standing in our polka-dot booth, I looked out and assessed

the companies around us. They boasted elaborate, custom displays that looked like they must have cost thousands of dollars. Some vendors occupied not just one, but two or three selling spaces. A seafood company near us displayed mixes for dips, stews, Bloody Marys, and more. A confectionary store stocked its enormous booth with every old-timey candy imaginable. I had no idea how we were going to entice buyers to come into our booth when there were so many options all around us—many of which looked much more impressive than our little one-product setup.

It was probably too late to be worried about how to sell, but I wasn't sure if Mom and I were prepared. *Are there keywords that get people to buy? If so, what are they?* All kinds of buyers would be here, representing everything from local pharmacies to independent gift shops to major chains like Crate and Barrel. We could find ourselves talking to mom-and-pop store owners from small southern towns or executives from New York—or just about anyone in between. *How are we going to know who's who and what they're looking for?* We needed to keep in mind that these people were not buying for their own consumption. They were buying for their customers. They were asking, "Can I make money selling this product? Is this product worthy of my brand and my customers?" When they sampled our cookie, they'd be judging much more than taste; they'd be evaluating our booth, our packaging, and us too. It was our job to decipher what they were thinking, to anticipate their questions, and to be ready to explain what made

Susansnaps unique and special. And we had only been doing this whole baking, packaging, and shipping gingersnaps thing for a hot minute. It was nice to have Nordstrom's coffee bars as our claim to fame, but other than that, we were about as green as they come.

Noticing I had become very quiet, Mom asked, "Sweetie, what's the matter?"

"I'm nervous we won't get to try out your carbon paper if we can't get anyone to stop. What if no one buys from us? Mom, what if this doesn't work?"

"The booth looks fantastic," she said. "We have plenty of samples. Everyone loves cookies."

"I know," I said, brushing off her enthusiasm. "But what are we going to say to people?"

Without hesitating, Mom responded, "We'll greet people, invite them to enjoy a sample, make them feel welcome to browse, and answer their questions. I'm sure whatever you say will be good." She paused. "It's not like we're selling vacuum cleaners or artificial topiaries. That would be a lot harder." Mom was right. It was easy to work on something we believed in. And as crazy as our gingersnap cookie company was, Mom and I did believe in it.

In trying to convince me that I could make this work, I think Mom was also trying to boost her own confidence. I chose to believe in her conviction, because we were stuck in that booth for the next three days, and it was either going to be one of the best or one of the worst experiences of my life.

Just then, a loud voice came over the intercom and said, "Welcome, exhibitors, to the September Atlanta International Gift and Home Furnishing Market. Buyers are lined up and waiting. It is now nine o'clock, and the doors are officially open. Have a great market!"

After the doors opened, we immediately heard pandemonium. I peeked out from our booth and looked down the aisle, spotting hordes of buyers coming our way. For a split second, I might have considered running away—but then I glanced at Mom. She looked lovely in her heels, black pants, and blazer. I was not about to let her down.

Before I knew it, people were streaming into our booth, and I was talking to them. "Hi, would you like to try a sample? Gourmet gingersnaps." I heard Mom greet another potential customer warmly. "Good morning! Please help yourself to a gingersnap." We must have been doing something right, because people were stopping at our booth, enjoying samples, and complimenting our decorative display.

When I eventually heard someone say, "I would like to place an order," I was stunned. *A what? An order? With us? Now?* A pleasant woman who owned a salon and spa in Athens, Georgia, wanted two cases of gingersnaps.

Mom, who was standing right next to me, was looking at me with wide eyes, nodding her head. "Susan, she'd like to place an order." As if I hadn't heard her myself. I was silently celebrating.

Okay, great. An order—this is good. We should have been doing something, but Mom and I were both just standing there. *Wait, this is my big moment.* I reached under the table, grabbed one of the clipboards, and handed it to Mom. We turned our backs to the buyer, which I'm sure is no-no in Selling 101, and Mom whispered, "Have you looked at this thing? How do I fill it out?"

Staring at a foreign spreadsheet crowded with boxes, numbers, and wholesale jargon, I told her, "It's no big deal." I had no idea what I was talking about. I had laid out the spreadsheet, but Dad had helped with the content, and our over-the-top order form was more intricate than necessary.

"Watch over my shoulder to make sure I don't mess up," Mom said.

It took all three of us (not just Mom and me, but the customer too) to finalize that first business deal, but after that, we were rolling right along. Mom was a natural saleswoman, and I couldn't help but think about how proud Aunt Sue would have been to see her little sister, Laura, selling and talking with customers. As for me, all I could seem to muster up was, "Would you like to try the ultimate gingersnap?" I lined up the carbon paper in between orders and answered any straightforward questions that people had. Over and over again, I parroted the same information— "Two case minimum…four-month shelf life…the bakery bag is the best value…tastes like the holidays"—while Mom took the more personal questions head on.

We soon learned that word spread quickly among the vendors when an executive from a large company or major chain of stores entered the building. That first day, a "suit" from T.J. Maxx came by and asked, "What do you have here? Your packaging is gorgeous."

Mom said, "We're Susansnaps—the ultimate gourmet gingersnap cookie. Please try one."

"You bake one cookie?" he asked. "Just this one?"

The smile on my face froze. I knew that only having one product would be a problem at some point. The man looked around our booth and nodded decisively. "Smart move. Don't overcomplicate. Do one thing and do it well. I like that. It shows confidence."

The compliment meant the world to us. Unfortunately, we weren't in a position to sell to him. We weren't a big enough operation. In fact, we hadn't really thought through how we would fill huge orders. The orders we filled for Nordstrom, less than two hundred cookies per store with just two or three stores ordering at a time, were small potatoes compared to what some customers at the Mart were buying. I guess we hadn't wanted to jinx ourselves by planning for high-quantity orders before we'd even gotten to the Mart.

It's funny how certain things have stayed with me. One person can make a difference without even knowing it. The conversation with the "suit" from T.J. Maxx reminded me of the technician at my first PET scan following treatment. I was terribly anxious (not about the test but rather the results), but my technician, Rodney, was so calm. By distracting me from the nuclear medicine he was injecting into me as well as the door covered with a "Do Not Enter: Hazard Zone" sign, he took me on a three-minute virtual escape to a Madonna concert in Miami he'd recently been to. His story was detailed, and I appreciated it.

For the rest of the show, Mom roped people in, and I filled out order forms and took payments. Mom was good at talking, and especially good at drawing people into the booth in the first place. My strengths lay more in writing and taking money. We made the perfect duo! We just slid into those roles naturally, and they've stuck ever since.

Fifty-six hours later, with a stack of papers beside me, I calculated that we had initial orders for 31,500 cookies, all of which would be made by hand. As Mom began dismantling our tables, I announced, "Looks like we're going to be busy." We received steady orders from then through the holidays.

Although I was having a lot of fun working with Mom, the bakery still didn't feel like a real job to me. But I never found the right moment to leave and pursue other opportunities. Something was always happening—a big order, an interview, a new show to attend, or an invitation to sell our cookies somewhere—and I didn't feel like I could leave Mom with all the work. So I would think to myself, *I'll just stick around until this is over.* And all the while, that black interview suit of mine was collecting dust.

Dear Sue,

I'm sure you never could have imagined it—Laura the salesperson! Believe me, neither could I. I don't know if this explanation makes sense, but I think this is what it came down to: whether I was at the wholesale market, a tiny craft show, or a speaking engagement (no kidding, I've done those too!), I found I cared so much about Susansnaps that I didn't care at all about messing up. I'd work as hard as I could and be as ridiculous as I had to be to keep Susan in this "thing" we had going. We were working hard and having fun, and it felt good. And it seemed like we just might be onto something. I wasn't going to let her down either. So just like I didn't care that I had to wake up in the middle of the night to help Susan when she was sick, I didn't care about calling out, "Please enjoy a gourmet gingersnap!" to compete with some guy passing out popcorn in the middle of a trade-show aisle right in front of us. He tried enticing buyers away from our booth, and I thought, Wait a minute. Two can play this game! *With a bit more gusto, I called out, "Susansnaps samples right here!" I would do whatever it took.*

14

Two Hands on Deck

EXHIBITING AT THE MART WAS SORT OF A REENTRY into the world for me. At home, I felt comfortable. My brothers and sister accepted me no matter what, and, of course, Mom and Dad did too. Although working for the first time since finishing treatment was a little scary, it was also invigorating and enlightening. And a lot more happened than just cookie sales over the course of those three days at the Mart. Since we couldn't leave our booth, even when there weren't any shoppers, I had time to think, observe, and reflect. I started noticing how I had changed, and I think Mom did too. Even though I kept thinking, *We don't know what we're doing here*, that wasn't quite true. If I could march into treatment and face my cancer day after day, then I could surely stand in a booth filled with cookies and sell them to customers.

It turned out that I didn't need to be so nervous about how

our product would be received at the Mart or whether we'd sell any cookies. Unconsciously, I began applying the same approach and outlook that I'd relied on during chemo and radiation. Just like with treatment, I soon learned that even though I didn't know how the show would turn out, there were a few things that I could control: I could choose to smile and be positive, to give it my all, and to appreciate each small success. Susansnaps never would have existed without my cancer, and as Mom and I stood in our booth, I realized, in some odd, backward way, going through treatment had prepared both of us to make this business successful. It had given us more inner confidence, greater drive. It was with this new strength that Mom would call out to buyers, "Help yourself to the ultimate gourmet gingersnaps! Anyone can have a gingersnap, but a Susansnap is unique." And, even though it was outside my comfort zone, I would sometimes speak up and try to sell to people too.

Mom and I were friendly and genuine and giving it our all, and somehow it was working. I think there was something about the two of us together that appealed to people. Even when we didn't know exactly what to say or how to close a sale, there was a certain effervescence coming from our booth. We believed in our product and believed in each other, and we figured if we were polite and had fun together, the rest would take care of itself. We were both aware that doing this right meant trying our best—the same way I had done my best during treatment.

Throughout the show, people commented on our positive attitudes. One evening, a vendor who we'd become friendly with came over and said, "Do you two always smile? I've been watching you. There have been no shoppers this afternoon, the place is practically dead, but you look like you're having the best time." The man, who sold frozen drink mixes, had been in the industry for years, and I'd assumed he was coming over to give us a pointer.

Caught off guard by his comment, Mom said, "What?"

"I just wanted you to know that if I were in the market, I'd buy whatever you're selling," he said. "You're doing a good job."

That was either the nicest compliment we'd had all day or a polite heads-up that we stood out like a sore thumb! Mom called back, "Thanks! We're happy to be here." And that was the truth. We had no reason to complain. Standing in a booth with no customers was better than lying in bed sick, wondering if the chemo was working. Sore feet or tired legs were better than excruciating bone pain or a burned throat. Since coming out of treatment, I'd become sensitive to people complaining. It bothered me. I'd hear vendors griping, "I don't like my booth location," or "The parking lot is too crowded," or "That buyer took too many samples and didn't order anything." Sometimes their trivial comments left me speechless. Other times I'd just say, "Hope your day gets better!"

People who visited our booth also commented on Mom and me working together. Some people thought it was great and said they'd love to work with their moms, but others, not so much. We kept hearing, "Are you mother and daughter?" and "You two work together?" and "You must be related. I can see it!"

Mom laughed. "It must be our matching blue eyes and blond hair!" Mom and I don't look alike. She has dark brown eyes and brown hair, while I have blue eyes and lighter hair. There must have been something in our mannerisms that made our relationship so obvious.

When people talked about how difficult they thought it would be to work with their mothers, Mom and I would look at each other and laugh, knowing exactly what the other was thinking. We had been through a lot worse than standing around in a booth together all day.

The show at the Mart proved two things: people liked our product, and Mom and I could push ourselves to accomplish our goals. We did something we'd never done before, and even though we were nervous, we kept going. And now that I knew we could do it, I was ready to do even more.

During treatment, when my only goal was to get through it, I had become used to taking things one day at a time, sometimes one hour at a time. But after our experience at the Mart, I saw the need to start planning for the future and strategizing about how to grow our business. Mom and I needed to think bigger.

Coming out of the show, we had more orders than we'd ever imagined we would—so many that it was difficult to get all the work done. Although gingersnaps were our specialty, we were still selling a range of other desserts, and it was getting tricky to juggle the different prep work and baking times for each product.

So while I was packing up boxes to ship out to customers one busy day, I asked Mom, "What if we put some of these desserts on the back burner? I've been thinking, maybe we should see what would happen if we focused solely on Susansnaps."

What I was proposing would be a huge leap of faith, and that was scary, but Mom agreed. "If we get any requests for cakes or pies, I'll bake them, but I'm game to stop promoting everything but the Susansnaps. Let's try it for a few months and see how it goes."

Laura's Divine Desserts remained our parent company, but from that moment on, we thought of our business as Susansnaps, and our signature gingersnap became our core product.

We'd learned at the Mart that most people selling at major wholesale trade shows don't make their products by hand. While most people had machines, suppliers, and warehouses, Mom and I had each other. From the dough to the packaging, our product was entirely handmade. That was another thing that set us apart, but I was beginning to see that if we wanted to grow our business, it wasn't going to be sustainable. We were working ridiculous hours, spurred on by the fear of having to call our new customers and say, *We're sorry for the delay, but your cookies won't be shipping on time.* Failure was not an option for us. Besides, the sooner we shipped orders, the sooner we'd get reorders. We had to figure out a way to be more efficient.

Our process of hand-scooping each individual cookie with a mini ice cream scoop produced perfectly round cookies, but it was laborious. We would start with a clump of cold dough in one pan and raw sugar crystals in another. Mom would scoop the dough, press it against the edge of the pan to flatten the top, then squeeze the lever on the ice cream scoop to release a little ball of dough into the second pan. From there, I would shake the ball of dough around in the sugar, then place it on a tray. We'd repeat that process sixty times, lining up the cookies ten across and six down. Then I would press the tops flat with the bottom of a glass measuring cup. Once we had five trays complete, they went into the oven, and twelve minutes later, perfectly round, toasty ginger-snaps came out, along with the wonderful aroma of ginger, cloves, and cinnamon.

One day, having lost count of how many trays we'd filled and baked, with my hand cramping up, I said, "Mom, there's got to be a better way. This is dumb."

Mom held up her hand in the shape of a claw and chuckled. "I think my hand's stuck like this. Can you unpeel my fingers?"

I did some research and found a machine called the Kook-e-King, which the manufacturer claimed would facilitate "low-cost automation of cookie production." Mom made some calls, finally connecting with a dealer in Illinois.

"Suz, do we want new or used?" she asked, holding one hand over the phone.

"Used?" I said. "I don't know. How bad are the used ones?"

"Well, the one this guy is selling has been refurbished and steam cleaned."

"Let's go with that, if we'll save a little money."

For the next few days, we continued making our gingersnaps the usual way, eagerly awaiting the delivery of the Kook-e-King. When it arrived, we discovered that it was surprisingly heavy. Mom tried to lift it and gasped, "Suz, grab the other side." We heaved it onto the table, and there it sat. All we had to do to get it running was attach one wire. We felt like we'd hit the jackpot.

"Grab a tray," I said. "Let's try this thing out."

Although "automation of cookie production" sounds fancy, the Kook-e-King basically worked like the plastic Play-Doh machine I used to have when I was little. You'd set the dough in the top of the machine, then slide a tray underneath it with your left hand while simultaneously turning a handle with your right. Six round discs of dough would drop in a single line across the cookie sheet. Then you'd slide the tray a bit more, turn the crank again, and six more discs would come out. It was very simple, but it was definitely a big improvement over hand-scooping each individual cookie. Mom and I were practically jumping up and down with excitement, fighting over who got to use it first.

"Okay, you go," I said to Mom. "I'll time you."

She grabbed the handle and started turning. *Crank, clink, drop. Crank, clink, drop.*

"Sixty cookies in seventeen seconds!" I announced. "Mom, just think how many we can do in a day!"

Susansnaps slowly grew over the next few months, morphing from something Mom and I had thought would be fun to try into a legitimate business. People tend to envision owning their own business as the most glamorous thing in the world, and sometimes it is, but most of the time, it's just a lot of hard work. We soon learned that *entrepreneur* was just a fancy French word that meant work! Since it was just the two of us, we got to spend plenty of time baking and chatting with customers, but we also had to take out the trash, wash dishes, mop the floor, work on the website, ship boxes, balance the books, and more. Every detail came down to us. It was exciting to watch Susansnaps grow, but sometimes it felt like a 24–7 job.

The best thing about Susansnaps was that our cookies made people happy. One order a day meant that we made one person smile. Four orders a day meant that we made four people smile. We weren't saving the world, but we had a product that made other people's day a bit better, and that drove us to keep going. Each day brought something new, and I started to enjoy that little bit of unpredictability. *Who will call today? How many boxes will we ship? What gift or food show will we be accepted to?* I couldn't wait to find out what would happen next. I loved imagining the possibilities, because I started to believe that every possibility was possible.

When we needed ingredients, we headed off to Costco. Doing our shopping was actually kind of fun, mostly because of the looks we'd get from other customers as we, this crazy mother-daughter duo, sped through the store at top speed, piling supplies onto a flatbed cart. We'd form our two-person assembly line, stacking up dozens of pounds of flour and sugar, hundreds of eggs, and so on. Then, to get the heavy flatbed in motion, Mom and I both had to lean our entire bodies into the handle and push, hoping that no innocent shoppers would wander into our path. With some maneuvering, we'd ease into the checkout line, where we'd get more looks and questions. "What could you two possibly be doing with all of this? Looks like you're going to be busy."

Mom and I would laugh. "Yep," we'd say, and we'd hand out a Susansnaps brochure for good measure.

One day, we inadvertently caused a bit of a scene. After we'd checked out, Mom ran to get the car while I waited with the flatbed. She pulled the car around and we began loading it, systematically stacking twenty-five-pound bags into the trunk. Just then, a huge fire truck pulled up behind us, casting a shadow over our car. A burly firefighter jumped out and called to us, "Do you two ladies need a little help?"

I wanted to say yes, but Mom answered, "Oh no, we've got it!" As if two women loading more than four hundred pounds of ingredients into a Volvo parked outside Costco was the most normal thing ever. That's Mom for you. Where there's a will, there's a way.

Another firefighter climbed out of the truck and laughed. "Really? We don't mind."

Mom responded, "Thanks, but we do this all the time. We're good."

"We could use you at the firehouse!" he said.

Once our car was stuffed, we slowly pulled away, riding what felt like two inches off the pavement.

.... ❧ ....

Things were going well for Susansnaps, so I thought it was time to take another shot at writing to newspapers and magazines about covering our story. I studied communication in college, so I had dabbled a bit with press releases. I knew to write in third person and keep it brief, fact-based, and to the point. I spent countless hours writing and rewriting our press release. But even though I'd followed the rules and included all the relevant information, something about what I'd written fell flat. It sounded impersonal, like I was writing about someone else. But I sent the press release out anyway, hoping that it would get other people interested in our story.

A few weeks went by with no response. I reread the press release over and over. It was grammatically correct, clear, and to the point, but I hated it. It sounded stiff. So I decided to try something different: I began writing a personal letter. I figured, *What's the worst that can happen? If it doesn't work, I'll try something else.* The letter came from me, and I felt much better about it. I wrote about my mom, Laura, and our cookie business called Susansnaps. I wrote, rewrote, tweaked, agonized over each word, and then finally thought, *Let's give this a whirl.*

For me, it was easier to write about our story than to tell it to customers in person. I wanted to share my thoughts about Mom, Aunt Sue, Dad, and myself, and I could write things that were hard to say out loud. I also knew that people weren't going to randomly discover our business or come up our driveway and magically find a gourmet cookie company at the end of it. Some media attention would help.

I planned to email the letter to Daryn Kagan, a former CNN news anchor who now ran her own website focusing on unique human interest stories that "show the world what's possible." Sitting in our office, I must have read my letter ten times over, to the point of driving myself nuts. Then I called upstairs to Mom, "I'm going to send it. Do you think I should? Should I read it to you again?"

Mom responded, "It's nicely written. I'm sure she'll like what you wrote. Send it."

I clicked Send. Less than seven minutes later, the phone rang. I assumed that it was Mom calling to tell me to come back upstairs. It wasn't. The caller ID read, "Kagan, Daryn." *This is a joke, right?* I jumped out of my chair and hovered over the phone. I didn't even know how to answer it professionally, since Mom took all the calls.

I picked up the receiver and tentatively said, "Hello?"

"Is this Susan?"

"Yes."

"Hi, it's Daryn Kagan. I'm looking at your email right now."

She's reading it now? While she's on the phone with me? Part of me was excited and part of me was mortified. As I panicked, she kept talking. "Thank you for your letter. I like your story, and I'd like to meet you and your mom. Are you available Tuesday?"

I gulped. "Yes, we are free Tuesday."

"Great!" she said enthusiastically. "I have your address. How about we make it ten thirty? See you then."

And that was that. *What just happened?* I thought. *I hit Send, and within ten minutes I got us an interview with a recognized journalist.* I ran upstairs to tell Mom, who asked the obvious questions: "What does she want to see? What is she going to ask us? What did she say?"

"Oh," I said. "I don't know. I didn't ask."

"Susan, you have to call her back and find out what questions she's going to ask so we can be prepared," Mom said.

"What?" I looked at her. "You think I should call Daryn back? Wouldn't that be weird?"

Mom shook her head breezily. "No. It's fine. You know she's at her desk right now, so just give her a quick call."

So I did. Can you believe it? I called her back and said, "Hi! It's Susan. I was wondering, what questions will you ask us? We want to be prepared." I bet I sounded ridiculous. Actually, I know I did.

Daryn was very nice. She might have chuckled a little, but she was reassuring. "I like to keep it fresh. I want to get your honest answers on camera. You'll be great. I'll guide you along."

But she didn't give us a list of questions. I still can't believe I called her. From then on, I never asked another reporter, journalist, or blogger to give us their questions ahead of time.

.... ❧ ....

In the meantime, I kept thinking. We didn't have funds to pay for traditional advertising, so we had to get creative. On one of our Costco runs, I brought our camera along. As we shopped, I flagged down another customer and asked him to take a picture of Mom and me loading our mountain of flour and sugar onto the flatbed. Then I wrote an email about how we buy all our supplies at Costco and sent it to their corporate office in Seattle. A few weeks later, a writer called. I took the phone out to our driveway, away from the hum of the oven and the buzz of the timer, answering questions. A month later, we had a nice mention in the *Costco Connection*—our first national publication. The West

Coast got the magazine first, and orders started popping up from Seattle, Portland, and San Francisco. I walked into the shop with a handful of printed orders from our online store and handed them to Mom. "Look! We've reached the West Coast."

Bolstered by our success, we decided to apply for the Yellow Daisy Festival, one of the largest outdoor craft shows in the South. We weren't sure what to expect, but some of the vendors we met at the Mart had highly recommended it, so we crossed our fingers that we would be accepted.

Mail came in the afternoons, and I started taking daily trips from the shop to the mailbox, hoping to find an acceptance letter. Trekking down our long, steep driveway, I couldn't help but notice how much easier it was to do, compared to a year ago. I used to take that same walk when I was sick, and I would have to stop and sit on the curb until I'd regained enough strength to walk back up. Now, as I zipped along effortlessly, I couldn't believe it used to take me twenty minutes, with the help of my sixteen-year-old sister, to get up and down the driveway. We would carry on like it was normal, chatting on the curb next to the mailbox. Carey would even wave at the cars that drove by, signaling *we're all good here*. By the time we'd shuffled our way back up, I would be exhausted. But the day the envelope arrived with Yellow Daisy Festival Jury stamped in the return address, I practically skipped back up to the shop.

A few months later, on the weekend after Labor Day, we

found ourselves at the show, standing under a white tent covering a dirt floor. Our tent was in the woods, nestled between two pine trees. It had drizzled that morning, and the air was extra steamy—not exactly ideal conditions for selling our cookies.

"Mom," I said, "do you think we should just pack it up and go?" I figured that nobody would want to buy gingersnaps on such a hot, muggy day, but Mom disagreed.

"Susan, we already paid for the booth. Let's just see what happens." She was right. We needed to sell enough to make up the cost of the booth and tent.

The Yellow Daisy Festival attracts many loyal vendors and shoppers who come back year after year. So when the entrance gate first opened in the morning, hundreds of early shoppers rushed past our booth, intent on visiting their favorite vendors. We stood under our tent and smiled, hoping that if we looked like we were having a good time, we'd draw some people in. As the day went on, thousands of shoppers flowed in and filled the pathways. We started offering free samples, raising our voices above the noise of the crowd to entice people into the tent to try our cookies.

Finally, a woman said, "These are so good. I'll take a bag." *One bag? One bag for nine dollars. This could be a long few days.*

I bent down to write a receipt for her, and by the time I straightened up, there were about twenty shoppers hovering around our table, waiting to pluck a sample cookie out of our big glass jar. We had a captive audience, and I thought, *There is no reason that any of these people should walk away from our booth without buying a bag of cookies.*

This crowd was different from the one at the Mart. These shoppers weren't business owners or corporate reps looking for new products to boost their bottom line; they were shopping for themselves or for their friends or loved ones. They were here for a more personal experience. Suddenly, I realized these shoppers were only aware that we were selling delicious cookies—they didn't know the bigger story behind Susansnaps. As Mom continued selling, calling out, "Baked fresh daily... Stay fresh four months," I lightly stepped on her foot. She stopped and looked over at me, making a face that clearly said, *What? Can't you see I'm busy?* I was too unsure of myself to speak up and tell our backstory, but I knew Mom could do it. With my foot still resting on top of hers, I said quietly, "Say something about *Susansnaps.*"

She looked around at the busy booth. "Right now?"

"Yes. Go for it. Look at all these people."

I figured if Mom gave a little spiel about Susansnaps and it wasn't well received, then fine, we wouldn't share it again. But I had a feeling people would be interested.

Mom cleared her throat and started speaking loudly, so that anyone who came near our tent would hear her. "Anyone can have a gingersnap," she began, "but a Susansnap is unique. This is a very special cookie. I owned a small dessert business, and then, unexpectedly, my husband and my daughter Susan both had to go through chemo at the same time. Ginger is a stomach soother, and cookies make people smile, so I baked about a hundred cookies to give away to the other patients at chemo."

As Mom continued, women walking by started tapping their friends' shoulders. "Did you hear that? Wait, listen to this story. This mom and daughter work together. They bake these cookies."

Mom drew a crowd around our table, and the funny thing at these shows is that when people see a crowd around a booth, they don't care what you're selling, they just want to get in on whatever is popular. One woman, waving her credit card in the air, called out from the back, "I'll take three bags," and just like that, shoppers left and right started pulling out their wallets. People bought our cookies as an afternoon snack for themselves, as dessert for the weekend, as gifts to save for Christmas, and even as something comforting they could give to friends or family members with cancer. We could barely keep up!

We got into a groove, and Mom told our story over and over as customers cycled in and out of our booth. Mom would reel folks in with samples. (Believe me, no one turns down a free cookie.) Once they were hooked on the delicious taste, she'd start telling our story. This went on for hours. Mom sold the cookies and I bagged them up, took the cash, and handwrote the credit card slips. We were nonstop busy. It was a good thing we'd eaten breakfast, because there was no time to stop and rest. But thankfully, we did have some bottled water. We both needed it when we started to lose our voices from calling out to the crowds so much. That was another thing—my throat. My voice would get weak, and projecting loudly would become difficult. I also had a swallowing issue due to the radiation treatment. It would flare up sporadically and was a nuisance. And then, I had this other random thing that was upsetting. Not only would I forget words, I sometimes struggled to get them out. Treatment aftermath. I guess that was part of the reason I was happy Mom was willing to call out to the crowd.

The sun was beating down on our tent, and with the sticky southern humidity, our booth felt like a hot sauna. The sun worked in our favor though. It was shining right on our sample jar and effectively rebaking our cookies, so that the smell of freshly baked gingersnaps wafted through the air, luring people into the booth. Mom and I continued to work together seamlessly, filling product, adding samples to the jar, selling, talking to customers, passing out brochures, and writing credit card slips. We were having a blast. And not because we were making money, but because we were pulling this off together, as a team.

The crowd was great, and we met all kinds of people. The feedback we were receiving was better than we could have imagined. Occasionally though, shoppers would say whatever came to their mind: "You haven't been in business very long, do you think you can make this work?" "That seems pricey for just some cookies." "Hodgkin's? You know that'll kill you." "I read somewhere that eating chicken causes tumors." Of course, it was the hardest to hear people weigh in on anything related to cancer. Mom suggested the best thing to do in those situations was to let the person say what they wanted to say, and then they'd move on.

The worst interaction of the show happened on the second day. I was on a selling high, all smiles, and went to help a man standing in the booth. Before I could get a word out, he said, "The government has a cure for cancer, they just won't give it to us because they make more money off people like you being sick and dying."

I didn't know what to say—I just stood there like a deer in the headlights.

He kept going. "It's population control. It's fine with the government that thousands of people die. There will never be a cure. Your cancer will probably come back. They just gave you enough medicine to get by."

By the time Mom realized I was in trouble, the crackpot had simmered down. She hurried over and asked, "Would you like to buy a bag or box?"

"No. I'm fine. Good luck to you," he said as he nodded to me and walked away.

I couldn't believe the terrible things he'd said to me. It was awful, and I hated the feeling of being backed into a corner. Mom wanted to know what he'd said. I started to tell her, but I didn't want her to get mad. And I didn't want to get upset. I turned my would-be tears into motivation. "Mom, we have work to do." I looked out into the crowd and took a deep breath. "Who would like a sample? These are Susansnaps. I'm Susan. This is a delicious and unique cookie…"

Mom and I never had a grand plan for how we were going to build Susansnaps. Honestly, one thing just led to another. Something would happen—a media pop, a show, a big order—that would help us go a few more months. There were certainly frustrating days, days when I thought about other things I might be doing with my life. Now that I was feeling better, I wasn't sure if or when I was supposed to go find a "real job." I agonized over whether I should pack it up and go on with the life I'd always imagined. But that life was gone. Somehow, without even realizing it, I had a new reality. I never could have imagined myself building a bakery business with my mom, but I loved the work and we were getting good at it. Whenever the voice in my head whispered, *But what are you* doing? I would just go back to the basics. I'd had cancer, and now I was baking cookies. And that was okay. It might not have been "normal," but, then again, what is normal anyway? My life might have been easier if everything had gone according to plan, but it would have been boring too. I would have missed out on selling cookies in the dirt with Mom!

Dear Sue,

When Susan was sick, I'd watch Carey lock arms with her and take her on walks. It was the sweetest thing ever. I would have done anything for you, so it was touching to see Carey step in so naturally and do the same for Susan. She knew instinctively what Susan needed, which was a comfort to me. Sometimes the two of them reminded me of us. I have hoped through the years that I was half the friend and sister to you that you were to me. My girls are inseparable. At times, it fills me with such joy seeing Susan and Carey together, and other times, it makes me long to hear your voice and laughter. It leaves a little hole in my heart. Sue, our relationship is irreplaceable.

15

For Better or Worse, in Sickness and in Health

YOU KNOW HOW THEY SAY YOU SHOULDN'T MARRY someone until you've seen them through a bad cold? Well, Randy and I had that covered. We might have been young, but we were wise beyond our years. Randy had sat in the waiting room with my parents and overheard the surgeon say, "It looks like cancer," and three years later, we were still good together.

One Friday evening, I got a call from Randy. "Hey, Suz, I got off work early. Want to grab dinner and watch a movie?"

I was happy to have a chance to hang out with Randy, although I was a bit confused about why he was off work, since he was bartending to help put himself through school and would usually try to pick up extra shifts on Friday nights.

But he'd said he was free for the night, so I ran out the door with my wet hair in a ponytail, wearing the first outfit I could find.

It was already getting late, and I had to get up early the next day to sell at an outdoor art festival, but I didn't think twice about it. No matter how often we saw each other, I never felt like I got enough time with Randy. There was never enough time. He had moved to Atlanta, and while his apartment wasn't far from me, he was very busy working two jobs and keeping up a full class schedule. Since getting sick, I'd become aware that life can change in an instant, so I started to appreciate the little things along the way. I made more of an effort to live in the moment, to relax and have fun.

I met Randy at a Mexican restaurant near his apartment, one of our favorites. We sat at the bar and had a beer, cheese dip, and tacos before going back to his apartment to watch a movie. I followed him in my car, but I could barely keep up as he sped down the streets. By the time I pulled into his parking deck, he'd already gone inside. I walked into his apartment, and the lights were off and the place was quiet. I called out, "Hey, Randy! Where are you?" Then I saw light shining under his bedroom door. Something was definitely up, but I had no idea what. I opened the door and saw roses and champagne and Randy down on one knee.

"What are you doing?" I exclaimed. "Are you for real?" Then, tugging on my old tank top, I said, "Look at me!" It was so ridiculous that it was actually perfect. We had talked about getting married, so a proposal wasn't entirely unexpected, but I was totally surprised by his timing.

"Susan," Randy said, "I can't imagine going through life without you. I want to spend every day with you. Will you marry me?"

I cried tears of joy, tears of laugher, tears of happiness. And I cried tears of heartache. Then Randy and I drove straight to my house, and I practically floated down the hallway to tell Mom and Dad.

We'd all known that Randy and I would eventually get married, but we hadn't known when or what kind of wedding we'd have. Between Dad losing his job and my piles of medical bills, I figured that a traditional wedding would be out of the question and thought we'd just do something small and simple. But my parents surprised us. Less than twenty-four hours after Randy's proposal, my idea of twenty people at the beach went out the window. Before Mom and I headed to the festival to sell cookies all day, Dad said to me, "You're getting married. There will be a wedding. A church, a priest, a venue, the whole thing."

I wasn't just surprised, I was overwhelmed. *This is too much. It's too generous. My parents have already given me so much.* But from the moment Dad said those words, Mom and I began talking, planning, dreaming, and having the most fun. I don't know why people say weddings are stressful or cause fights. I wasn't going to flip out over deciding between white, silver, or monogrammed cocktail napkins. I knew there were much bigger things in life to worry about.

I think we all viewed the wedding as a sign of moving on, moving toward the future. But it was also true that by marrying me, Randy was agreeing to take on my past and its implications on the future. There would be years of follow-up visits with Dr. Weens and routine PET scans. There would be medical bills and the looming, unspoken threat of the cancer recurring. I also had to pay extra-close attention to my health. If I went to the doctor for a cold, they would do blood work. If I got a bad headache, they'd order a scan. If I had trouble swallowing because of the damage that radiation had done to my throat, they'd send me to the hospital for an endoscopy. But Randy never minded, or at least, he never showed me that he did.

When I started sharing the news that I was getting married, people had all kinds of reactions, from the standard "I'm happy for you" to the less congratulatory, "Really? To whom?" or "When did you meet him? How long has he known you?" I got what people were hinting at. Why would anyone sign on to all this? I never thought of myself this way, but I eventually realized some people in the outside world saw me as damaged goods.

But Randy and I talked about everything, and we'd had conversations I don't think most twentysomethings have had. When we had to go to marriage classes and they asked each couple to decide who would take out the trash and wash the dishes, Randy and I laughed. If chores were our biggest challenge, then we were going to be just fine.

A major perk of owning your own business is that you are your own boss and you can set your own schedule. That came in handy after I got engaged. Mom and I worked quickly and at odd hours so that we could check out wedding venues, visit dress shops, and meet with florists during the day. I didn't have a binder full of ideas that I'd been saving for years or a grand vision of exactly what I wanted. I just wanted a nice day, a pretty dress, and Randy to be waiting for me at the end of the aisle.

But I was set on three specific things for the wedding: I did not want any crying, I did not want to use Susansnaps as reception favors, and I would carry red roses. As Mom and I stood around our shop table working on our baking assembly line, with the oven timer buzzing every ten or twelve minutes, we discussed these things.

"Mom," I said, "I don't want anyone crying at the wedding. It's a good day. A happy day."

"All right," she replied. "But it could be emotional; there might be a few tears."

I looked at her. "No, I really don't want that. Cry now if you have to. Get it out. We've had plenty of bad days with tears, but this is not going to be one of them. If you start crying, or Dad, or me, then everyone will be crying. I really don't want that."

Mom was right, of course. It would be an emotional day.

Weddings generally are emotional, but this one would be slightly more so. I knew there had been a time when Mom worried about whether Dad would even be alive to walk me down the aisle, but I just didn't want to cry on my wedding day. I was so afraid that if we started crying, we wouldn't stop. I also didn't want that moment to be about cancer, about chemo or the two of us surviving or anything related to our health. I felt very strongly that if one tear was shed, it would look like we were crying over cancer. I wanted the wedding to be about Randy and me getting married, and nothing else.

We picked out the music for the church ceremony very early on. Mom and I went through a variety of songs before we landed on the one that would play while Dad and I walked down the aisle. It was a regal instrumental song, and I ordered it on CD for Mom. She told me later that she'd listen to it over and over again in her car when no one was with her and think about Dad and me coming down that aisle. She said there were plenty of times that she sat at red lights sobbing.

As funny as it may seem, I was adamant about not wanting to have Susansnaps at the reception. They may be delicious, and everyone does love cookies, especially as a party favor; in fact, we'd sold them to many brides. But I was not going to be one of them. I didn't want to mix my work with my wedding, and I didn't want the ginger cookies Mom had first made when Dad and I were going through chemo to be part of such a joyful day.

Instead, Mom and I made what we called pecanies—buttery pecan cookies we hand-rolled into little balls, baked, and then tossed in powdered sugar. Each guest would leave with cookies, just not our specialty gingersnaps.

The last point I was really set on was the flowers. From the time I was little, I loved looking at pictures of Aunt Sue in Mom's collection of family photos. I was completely captivated by her and would try to find physical similarities between us or something to link us together besides sharing the same name, but there was nothing. Aunt Sue had gorgeous honey-brown hair; smooth, pale skin sprinkled with freckles; a distinct twinkle in her eyes; and the most beautiful aura. I always wanted to know what she was thinking.

I especially loved looking at her wedding photo. I'd ask, "Mom, why does she have red roses?" The day of Aunt Sue's wedding, the florist showed up with the flowers, and when Aunt Sue opened the box that held her hair wreath, she was shocked and disappointed to find red roses, not the white ones she had ordered. It was too late to replace them, so Aunt Sue wore the wreath of red roses. The rich red flowers were so beautiful against the soft curls of her light brown hair and her ethereal white wedding gown. It wasn't what she'd wanted or asked for, but she'd made it work, and she looked perfect. I always liked that story because it said so much about Aunt Sue. I knew from an early age that someday, when I got married, I would carry red roses just like hers.

Ten months passed, and before I knew it, the church was filled with ninety-four of our closest family and friends. Mom, my brides-maids, Dad, and I were in the back of the church waiting to walk down the aisle. As the organist started playing, my heart began to pound. Dad and I stood off to the side, trying to stay out of sight. This was the church we'd gone to every Sunday as a family, where I went to elementary school, and now, where I'd get married.

Mom came over to Dad and me. "You look beautiful. I can't wait to see you two walk down the aisle."

I felt my eyes brimming with tears. I didn't say anything back, but I gave a huge smile as Dad told her, "Laura, you'll miss your cue. See you at the end of the aisle."

Finally, it was down to Dad and me. Just the two of us. It was an emotional moment, but I didn't want to cry. Instead, my left arm began shaking uncontrollably. Dad laughed as I showed him my trembling arm, and I couldn't help but laugh a little too.

Even though I didn't want to think about all we'd been through, it was impossible not to. Dad looked great in his tuxedo, so happy and calm. I just thought, *We did it. We made it. We're both here.* I was excited to get to the end of the aisle and stand next to Randy. But right then, in that moment, I was bursting with pride to be arm in arm with Dad.

Dad and I made our way to the center of the vestibule. The organist switched songs, the trumpet began heralding, the guests stood up, the church doors opened, and I thought my heart was going to leap out of my chest. Dad and I stood there and smiled.

My left arm was still shaking. It was a long aisle…a very long aisle. I could feel tears coming. For a second, it all sank in—everything that had happened to lead us here. Not to mention that I could see Dr. Weens sitting off to the side. I was able to fight back the tears, but in the process I'd stopped walking. I whispered to Dad, "Please stop."

He looked over at me. "Are you okay?"

I nodded. "One minute."

After a few seconds, he said, "Are we ready to go?"

I turned my face forward and whispered, "Not yet."

The church was enormous, a large, ceremonial sanctuary. My eyes locked onto the gold crucifix up by the altar. I'd walked up and down this aisle on countless Sundays throughout my life. But it had never been just Dad and me, arms linked together. I thought again, *We are here. I am here. Dad is here.* Dad was filled with joy and life that day. I wanted to take it all in. I chanted in my head, *This is a good day.*

Dad said, "Susan, I've got you." To me, it felt like this pause lasted minutes, but it was all of five seconds. Five seconds I will always remember.

Finally, I nodded my head and off we went. Dad and I glided down the aisle. Randy and I had the most wonderful day. This was a blissful moment. This was a celebration.

Dear Sue,

I was thrilled to be a bridesmaid at your wedding. You had such a great time planning every detail. I loved wearing the pale-blue dress you chose with delicate embossed white butterflies scattered across the fabric. And, Sue, you looked so pretty. Your face was radiant. I had never seen you happier than you were that day. Susan's wedding day was equally wonderful.

It wasn't long after Ken was diagnosed that Mother and Dad came for a visit. Dad said he wanted to ride with me to pick up Robert from high school. He did, but he also wanted to talk with me alone about Ken's cancer. He worried for me in not knowing what the future would bring, saying, "You must feel like there is a sword over your head and you don't know when it will fall."

Through the years I've thought countless times of that heartfelt talk with Dad and realized he was perhaps describing how he and Mother felt worrying about you. Not only worried about when you'd be sick again but living with knowing you would die young. It must have been more difficult than I can imagine for them to hear you say to Hoxsie during your vows, "Unto death do us part," wondering when that would be.

There was a time when I was terrified. Will Ken live to see our kids grow up, graduate from high school and college? Will he live to walk his daughters down the aisle?

I didn't know I'd end up having to worrying about Susan living to see that day too.

Seeing Ken and Susan emerge from the back of the church was glorious. Leaning into the aisle to get a better look, they about took my breathe away. It was a sight I will never forget.

Following Susan's wishes, I shed no tears that day. But that didn't mean I hadn't shed a few leading up to the wedding. I would only let myself cry when I was alone in the car. And, it wasn't about seeing her in a wedding dress or her fluffy veil. What if, after Susan moved out, something happened to her and I wasn't there? I had been looking out for her every single day since she started her treatments. What would it be like not being fully responsible for her? Sue, I didn't like the cliché, "Now she can be somebody else's worry. Aren't you glad to get rid of her?" I wasn't. It was difficult to think of her driving down the street to another house. Although she used to joke about having to still live at home with her parents, Ken and I were happy to have her there with us. I had a watchful eye on everything. If she looked pale or tired, I was there. Checkups and scans, I was there. And, even though the treatments were over now and things were good, I still had my fears. I knew the cancer could come back.

If I could have chosen to spare Randy the sadness I know he felt in seeing Susan suffer and his worries of what could happen to her and what their future might be, I would have.

But I could see for myself what Susan meant to Randy, and that brought me great comfort. I reached over to hold Ken's hand in the church pew as we witnessed Randy and Susan exchange vows. And I'd be lying if I didn't say I couldn't help but think of Mother and Dad.

16

No Guts, No Glory

IT WAS A GOOD THING MOM AND I HAD CABLE IN THE shop so we could watch our lineup of shows. Spring was a slower time for us, and that year the economy was going into the gutter. Each day it seemed like the news about the bad economy got worse and worse, until one day the news anchors announced, "The United States is in the worst recession since the Great Depression." It was distressing for a lot of reasons, not least of which was that a recession was definitely not good for our budding cookie business. It felt like the anchors were speaking directly to us: *It's not an ideal time to have a home-based business. No one is going to buy from you. No one in America should be buying anything.*

The situation became depressing and terribly worrisome. We wouldn't say anything to each other while the news was on. Some days we even pretended not to hear the news at all. But there were times that our lunch conversation would end with, "What are we going to do? Is it over?" We decided that just because it was becoming harder didn't mean we were going to quit. If anything, the challenges just fueled us to be more creative and to come up with new ideas for drumming up business. The bottom line was that we needed to sell cookies. We needed orders. Simple. But how could we reach new people and convince them to buy?

Mom and I would stand in the shop and strategize. "If we sold at least a few boxes a day right now, we'd make it to the holidays… If our website attracted more shoppers… If some of our gift stores placed really large wholesale orders…" Those were a lot of ifs, and we knew it. We couldn't keep sitting there hoping business would come to us. Looking back, I can't believe all the things we pulled off, tried, and did. Our challenging times didn't last long, but they had a lasting effect. They made us tough. I became daring in a way. Not that I'll swim with sharks or jump out of an airplane, but I'm willing to try and push myself in a new way. Where I might have seen obstacles before, now I saw opportunities. Mom and I decided to say yes to different kinds of opportunities, yes to any and every idea we could dream up, and yes to recommendations and suggestions from our customers, other business owners, and even our friends. Sometimes they worked, other times they didn't, but we were in it together, and that made it easier.

One big change we made was introducing new flavors of Susansnaps. Up until that point, we'd sold only one cookie, our traditional gingersnap, but we did some experimenting and came up with two additional flavors: chocolate and lemon gingersnaps. We had never seen anyone else do flavored gingersnaps, and the recipes we devised were delicious. So we thought, *Why not give it a try?*

We also decided to take Susansnaps on the road for years, attending as many shows as we could. Sometimes we had great success and other times we bombed; with each show, we never knew exactly what to expect. We went to a very popular Christmas gift show in Nashville, Tennessee, attended by thousands of shoppers. It took us two years of applying to get accepted, but once we were finally there, we couldn't get one single, solitary person to stop at our booth. We had no idea why, and it wasn't for lack of trying, but we only made a few sales. Do you know how depressing it is to drive home from a long show with a van full of product? I was tempted to tell Mom that we should just dump it on the side of the freeway. Every box that rattled on the way home was a reminder that we had failed.

When Nordstrom asked us to set up a booth in our local mall, we did, basically putting up a card table and trying to sell to weekend shoppers. We went to farmers' markets on Saturday mornings, trying several neighborhoods around Atlanta. At one, we only sold three bags of cookies, making twenty-seven dollars in sales against our forty-dollar entrance fee. I could go on and on about our various show experiences, like the time we sold in a horse stall inside a barn, and yes, there was old horse poop in the corner. Or the time we went to a show that was actually a carnival, complete with cotton candy, funnel cakes, and Ferris wheels. At least our local fire department was happy when we didn't sell product—they got a lot of free cookies. It was either them, the cancer center, or the food bank. We couldn't let our unsold cookies go to waste.

Other times, we had more sales than we could handle. We went to the holiday sale at Bizarre Bazaar, a popular gift show in Richmond, Virginia, and were given a prime booth. Right from the opening of the first day, people kept stopping by, telling us they loved our story. It took us a while to figure out they already knew about us because we'd been featured in the *Richmond Times-Dispatch* that morning.

By the last day of the show, we had completely sold out. We'd never sold out on the road before. If we ran out of cookies at a show near our shop, we'd just get up early in the morning or have someone fill in at the booth while we baked more. Here, there was nothing we could do but offer to take orders and ship them for free, in hopes of capturing some of the lost opportunity. Some shoppers were not so pleased, complaining, "I heard about you and wanted to buy these. You don't have any more? Are you kidding?" At one point, Mom said to me, "Go to the van and see if you can find any! Maybe some slipped under the seats?"

One woman even leaned over our display table to see if we were hiding any cookies. On our way home, Mom said, "If we could have sold the polka dots off our tablecloths, people would have bought them from us." We were thrilled that Susansnaps had been such a success.

When we were out on the road, my main job as the navigator was to find the closest Cracker Barrel to wherever we were heading. A trip wouldn't have been complete without a dinner or two at Cracker Barrel. One time, we were driving home late at night and stopped at a Waffle House on the side of the freeway in a not-so-pleasant neighborhood. We had $6,000 in cash on us. Mom didn't think it would be smart to leave it in the van and said, "Suz, grab the cash."

"How much? Just for dinner?"

"No. All of it. Stuff it in my purse. We're taking it with us."

I wadded up the $6,000. And with that, we went in for our $2.99 waffles and scrambled eggs!

If Dad or Randy knew some of the things we did, they'd be so mad at us! So we didn't tell them. This wasn't to deceive—it was our optimism. Mom and I had a pact between us since the get-go: "No matter what happens, we say it went well." Every event we went to or sale we attempted, that had been our deal.

.... ❧ ....

One of our infamous trips was to Palm Beach, Florida. After twelve hours of driving, we were pulling off the freeway when Mom said, "Susan, grab the directions. Which way do I go?"

"This says turn right."

"Okay, but I'm pretty sure West Palm Beach is to the left."

We turned right, and I wondered, *Is Mom seeing what I'm seeing?* as we drove past barbed wire and armed guards.

Hesitantly, Mom said, "Is that a prison?"

"Um. Yeah, I think so." As we pulled into the parking lot for our venue across the street, I couldn't help but add, "Is anyone going to come to this event?"

The show started off very slow. The air-conditioning had broken, so it was extremely hot. And no one was shopping. The aisles were quiet. Other vendors began complaining among themselves, but Mom and I would have nothing to do with that.

The ticket price for this event included admission to see some famous chefs from the Food Network do cooking demonstrations, which seemed to be the main attraction for the show—the crowds for those events were enormous.

As Mom chatted with some shoppers, Ashley, the coordinator of the show, ran up to our booth with a giant grin on her face. She blurted out, "Bobby Flay likes Susansnaps! Out of all the food here, he likes your cookies best. He wants to know if he can use them in his cooking demonstration."

We had offered bakery bags for the backstage celebrity lounge but didn't think much about it.

"Is that okay?" Ashley prompted.

"Yes! Of course," Mom responded quickly. "He didn't have to ask, but thank you for letting us know."

Ashley started to walk away, waving frantically for me to follow her, so I did.

Before I could ask where we were headed, Ashley pulled back a long black curtain. There was Bobby Flay, sitting in an armchair in the middle of a makeshift greenroom, holding a white bakery bag with a familiar black-and-white polka-dot ribbon. Bobby Flay was eating our snaps. *Wow. A famous chef is eating something Mom and I baked*, I thought.

Ashley introduced us. "Bobby, this is Susan. She's the one who makes the gingersnaps." Bobby got out of his chair and stuck out his hand to greet me.

After I ceked out a profound, "Hi! I'm Susan," I saw a woman wearing a headset peek between the curtains.

"We're ready," she called.

Bobby Flay glanced at the bag in his hands. "These are delicious. Nice work."

"Thank you," I said. "My mom and I bake them. We turned our garage into a commercial kitchen, and we can bake up to five thousand in a day."

He smiled. "You and your mom? You bake these cookies?"

As he began moving toward the exit, I heard Mom's voice in my head: *Say something.* I was still surprised, but I took a breath and said in a rush, "Yes, we do. We only bake gingersnaps. My dad and I both went through chemo. My mom had started a dessert company, and she heard that ginger was a stomach soother, so she created this recipe, and now we work together."

He stopped walking and looked right at me. "That's fantastic," he said. "You've got a good thing going. You two keep baking." And that was it.

I was bursting with excitement when I got back to the booth, but there was no time to tell Mom the details, because word had gotten out that we had "the Bobby Flay cookies," and customers were swarming our booth. We were told that during his dessert demo, Bobby said, "Why bake when you can buy Susansnaps?" and he shared a snippet about us.

It was fantastic that a famous chef had given our product the thumbs-up. But the thing we took away from this? You never really know what's going to happen until you show up.

After a failed show or multiple days without orders, it was the messages we received that encouraged us to keep going.

"Hi, Mary! Sending love, hugs, prayers, and good karma! Along with some yummy cookies. Much love."

"Grandma, happy birthday! I'm thinking of you, and I wish I could sit down with you and eat these cookies!"

"Dave, never give in! Never give up! I hope these cookies give you strength to fight. You've got this, and we love you."

I'd think, *Who else can we reach? It can't be over until we've exhausted all possibilities. We can do this.* And we did. There would be one person in Wyoming sending a cookie gift to their friend in Nebraska. Somebody in North Carolina shipping to Arizona, and in the meantime, thanking us for having this cookie company.

In the midst of all the things we were trying, I also realized I had one life, and I needed to make the most of it. That's what we were doing with Susansnaps, and I felt like I was bringing Aunt Sue along too. Mom, Aunt Sue, and I were in this together. Whenever we tried something new, Mom and I would figure, *What's the worst that can happen?* If we got turned down, something didn't work, or we got no response, I could live with that. We wouldn't know unless we tried.

We started doing speaking gigs as well. We'd speak to groups of twenty and groups of two hundred: church, high school, ladies clubs, bereavement groups, rotary clubs. We weren't beyond cold calling either. We never had appointments, but we'd deliver cookies to radio shows in the wee hours of the morning, companies around town, car dealerships, doctor and dentist offices, yoga studios, veterinarian offices, CPAs, and lawyers. Is it possible to feel totally confident and insecure all at the same time? I did. But my inner drive pushed past that. It had to in order to keep up with Mom. She takes things on with gusto. I would walk into a front office and say, "Hello, I have a delivery," all the while thinking, *What am I doing?* And Mom would give her best, "Are you familiar with Susansnaps? We thought you'd like to know..." Even if someone wasn't too sure about us, the offer of free cookies got us in the door.

The worst, but also the best, was when we'd get to an office complex and we'd get out of our car and go separate ways. "Suz, I'll go to the building on the right," Mom would say. "You go that way." Oh, I loved and hated this. Mom and I would meet back at the car with all kinds of stories.

I continued writing to newspapers, radio, TV shows, and magazines. Big news, little news, and everything in between was important to us. Mom and I found ourselves plopping on headsets for an interview with Atlanta Business Radio. I was grateful to have gotten a call to be on, but once we sat down with a gigantic microphone two inches from our faces, I sort of wanted to escape. This was going to be live, and any bloopers would be recorded.

Then we came up with the craziest idea we'd had yet. We decided to fly to New York to hand deliver letters and cookie samples, in hopes of getting in a major magazine.

As Mom and I stood on a busy sidewalk in Manhattan, I began to question why we had thought this was a good idea. Standing among street vendors selling hot dogs and jumbo pretzels, taxis buzzing up and down Eighth Avenue, and businesspeople coming and going, the two of us with our boxes of Susansnaps suddenly seemed trivial. Once again, I found my heart pounding, my palms sweating. *What will we say? What's going to happen?*

Staring into the large, pristine lobby of the Hearst Corporation's headquarters, I'd be lying if I didn't say I was apprehensive. But I believed we had a product, a company, and a story this media empire should know about, so I reminded myself, *It's just a glass door to a building in a city. You know you've got this.*

I had this thing I learned to do when I thought something was too much for me or when I was nervous and unsure: *inner pep talks*. My chemo had an accumulative effect, where each round was more difficult. It became harder knowing what was coming. When I rode the elevator to treatment, my heart would start pounding, my palms would sweat, and I'd begin to panic. I dreaded knowing that in a few minutes I would have to step off the elevator and surrender myself to more chemicals, more sickness, and more pain. But I would build myself up: "You can do this. You can step off this elevator. And, look, Mom's right there next to you." With a deep breath and a smile, I'd step off the elevator. If Mom and I could do that, we could certainly do this.

We didn't have any appointments. No one knew we were coming. Maybe it was crazy, but I let myself be proud of us for at least showing up and trying.

"Mom," I said. "What are we going to do?"

"Look confident and act like we know what we're doing."

So that's what we did. We marched over to the front desk and Mom said, "Yes, we have deliveries to make to O magazine, *Redbook*, and *Woman's Day*," figuring the men behind the desk would let us through the secure turnstile. I bet we gave the security personnel a good laugh. They didn't let us go up to the offices, but they did kindly point us in the direction of the delivery station and mail room around back.

We delivered letters on two different occasions, and on a third trip to New York, we were invited to stop by and say hello at *O* magazine and *Redbook*, both of which had already published blurbs on us. That time, we had appointments, and we were warmly welcomed.

There have been times when we've been working that I've thought, *This is crazy. All of this. That we even do this.* And in the midst of Mom's and my chatter, laughter, and efforts, I can't help but think, *I love working with Mom. I can't believe what we went through and are now pulling off.* And when there is a bad show, no sales, dissatisfied customers, or just an off day, Mom and I can honesty look at one another and say, "It's just cookies." And we both know exactly what that means.

Dear Sue,

How many times have I thought, If you could see me now? *Certainly one of them would have been me walking down Peachtree Street in Atlanta dragging a tent on wheels behind me at 7:30 a.m. to set up for the Green Market. Sometimes Susan and I had to divide and conquer tasks, and this time, I drew the short straw for the Saturday morning farmers' market. I found myself going back to the car multiple times for our folding table, banner, samples, and product, only for a summer thunderstorm to arrive thirty minutes in. I could hear your "Oh, just leave it!" as I packed up and ran each load back to the car. In that moment, I wanted to call Susan and say "I quit."*

This one I couldn't believe. I answered the phone one afternoon to hear a pleasant woman tell me she was calling from Martha Stewart Living. *When she used my name I thought,* I'm getting a personal call about a magazine subscription? *She called to notify Susan and me that there were ten stories selected from across the country for their Dreamers into Doers Awards and that Susan's letter was one of them. I must have sounded baffled because she added, "I promise, this is not a come on." I was baffled! I had no idea what she was talking about, and Susan was on a week-long vacation in California.*

When I reached Susan, I barely started to tell her about the call when she began laughing and repeating over and over, "Are you kidding me?"

I had to wait until Susan regained her composure to find out what she had done. "What did you write?" I asked.

"I don't remember. I didn't save it. I wrote about you. They were looking for women who've turned their dream into something. What did the lady say?"

Sue, back in the seventies, Martha Stewart was coming on the scene as a professional caterer and hostess extraordinaire. Since then, she has become a media mogul known for her expertise in cooking, decorating, and entertaining. So now you can understand Susan's reaction.

Susan and I were treated to a two-day affair with plane tickets, rides in stretch limos chauffeuring us around Manhattan, a shopping spree, and a chic hotel with great views of the city. Everything Martha Stewart and her team did for us was top-notch. And we were honored at their awards gala in beautiful Lincoln Center. Our pictures—yours too—were shown on a giant screen while Susansnaps was being highlighted.

As for Martha, we were sipping champagne at the cocktail party when we got a chance to be personally introduced. In meeting her, I said, "Thank you for this lovely recognition. I'd like you to meet my daughter Susan."

Guess what she said! "Well, of course, you can't have a Susansnap without a Susan," Martha said in her precise diction. "It's a pleasure to meet you both."

Martha was exactly what I hoped she'd be like. She was stunning—head to toe perfection. You would have loved her attention to detail. Everything from the flower arrangements to the hors d'oeuvres to the private dinner we attended later in the evening was flawless. Susan and I had enjoyed every minute.

PS Sue, remember the Tapestry album we sung our hearts out too? I met her. I met Carole King at this event. She was being honored with "The Living Legend" award. And she didn't disappoint. She played "You've got a Friend" on a gorgeous grand piano, and I about lost it. When she sang, "Close your eyes and think of me and soon I will be there..." I was so moved that I had to pinch myself to keep the tears in.

17

Open for Business

WE HAD TAKEN SUSANSNAPS AS FAR AS WE COULD IN our garage kitchen. It was time to move out. Mom and I realized if we wanted to grow, we needed retail space. There's something official about having a commercial address and a brick-and-mortar store. Although our current shop was accessible, it was also on our home property. That meant if someone wanted to pick up an order on a Saturday morning, they might pass my dad mowing the lawn or encounter one of my siblings backing down the driveway. We were closed for pickups on Sundays and Mondays, but that didn't stop people from knocking on the front door of our house. We also had to park our cars strategically to make sure that customers could turn around. In addition to those inconveniences, the higher cost of residential shipping was eating away at our bottom line. And when the weight of a freight truck crushed a portion of our driveway one day, that was it—we decided that we had to move.

Having a store would also mean we could stop renting cargo vans, stuffing them with gingersnaps, and driving all over the South to attend shows. Instead, we could let shoppers come to us, and as far as I was concerned, that day couldn't come soon enough. I was ready for our days of being on the road to be over!

The next thing I knew, we were peering into the window of a hole-in-the-wall retail space. I asked Mom, "Are we really doing this?" but it was too late; I could tell that heavenly music was going off in her head. Mom loved it. Me, not so much. It was a run-down space in an old building on a side street in Atlanta. But it was all we could afford. Looking through the dirty window, I could see filthy brown carpeting, stained ceiling panels, and walls covered with pegboard. It wasn't set up for baking or selling food. Honestly, I wouldn't have wanted to eat anything that came from that space.

Mom said, "It might need a little work." That was an under-statement. But we both agreed to it, snatching it up without even stepping through the door or having a contractor look at it—and without knowing that it didn't even have a toilet or a sink.

Mom loved this dismal spot, and although I had my doubts, I was going to have to trust her conviction on this one. It was a done deal; this was going to be our new headquarters. Mom and I had gotten through personal challenges. This was a professional challenge. And I knew we had it in us to push ourselves. It was uncanny how much our experience with cancer had prepared us for creating, running, and growing our small business. Here, as we had in so many other ways, we took a leap of faith.

All the tradesmen in town, from a young, hotshot builder to a crew of veteran contractors, sized us up as a sweet mother-daughter team and gave us bids so outrageously priced I thought they'd added an extra zero by mistake. Little did these contractors know, Mom had renovated houses, so she recognized that their numbers were patronizing and unfair. And Mom didn't like that. She said, "If you want something badly enough, make it happen."

I couldn't agree more. That special, "only-I-can-do-that-for-you," durable floor-sealing job we were quoted $3,700 for turned out to be nothing more complicated than a trip to Home Depot, $257 for paint and sealant, and a little elbow grease before Mom and I had done it ourselves. There was something satisfying in starting from scratch and taking charge. We subcontracted the renovation, hired Randy and Luke for backup, and did whatever was left ourselves, including arranging all the necessary permits, inspections, and codes. Soon enough, we had turned the drab, dingy little storefront into the cutest polka-dot cookie emporium, and we couldn't have been more excited.

Our loyal customers were just as thrilled as we were, and we were all counting down the days until the store opened. But with progress came setbacks too. A big storm came through and flooded our store. Rain poured down from the roof and blew sideways through the cracks around the bricks. It was a swampy mess.

Shortly after we got that cleaned up, we visited Coca-Cola's corporate offices, selling cookies at their in-house employee holiday shopping extravaganza. While we were there, our new storefront sign was being put up. We had approved the design and were ready for it to start announcing to the city, "We're here!" But when we returned to the store and drove past the shop to check out the sign, I cringed at the sight of it.

"This is embarrassing," I said.

Mom agreed. "Well, isn't that something? It makes it look like we didn't have enough money to get a grown-up sign."

We pulled into our parking lot and got out to take a closer look. It was too small. The font was minuscule. The sign was barely noticeable, the words were hardly legible, and the worst part was that this had been one of the few things we'd allowed ourselves to have done for us, and it wasn't done right.

I wanted to believe the sign was okay. "The white background looks bright and clean, Mom," I said. But it didn't look great, grand, or special at all.

No matter how much time we put in, there always seemed to be one more thing that still needed to get done, and everything took longer than we thought it would. We only had one oven, so we had to strategically plan what day to shut it down, take it out of the garage, and move it. That involved hiring movers, a handyman to drill a hole in the wall to connect the exhaust pipe, and an electrician to hook it up, as well as timing everything so that we could resume baking within twenty-four hours. It was November, just heading into the busy holiday season, and we were taking orders, baking, filling orders, and shipping every day; we could not afford to pause. We set an opening day for the new store but pushed it back once, twice, until we just had to say, "We're unlocking the door tomorrow." If we didn't open, we'd miss the holiday rush.

.... ❧ ....

It was two o'clock in the morning, and we were opening in eight hours. Mom and I went to the twenty-four-hour FedEx Office to laminate our price signs. I doubted that such a small detail would make or break our first day, but by then, we were delirious and felt like we had to get it done. As I ran the signs through the laminating machine, one of them got jammed. The paper started going in crooked, and the machine began making clicking sounds.

Mom hurried over. "What did you do to this thing?"

"I didn't do anything!" I answered, slightly frantic. "It's the machine. It just started eating it or something."

Mom began wrestling with the machine. "Hold on. I'll get it out." She pulled on the paper with all her might, then started laughing.

"Mom, this isn't funny!" I was giggling now too. "How much does one of these things cost? We're going to have to buy it."

I doubled over and Mom started crying, she was laughing so hard. We were dog-tired and so excited that we were halfway between laughing and sobbing. Then we noticed that the machine was smoking.

There were no people around, no cars on the streets. Everything was quiet and still, and it was just the two of us in the middle of the night. How many late nights had we been up together, dealing with the side effects of treatment? It was an odd moment. We'd been working so hard on the new store that we were drained. It was physically tiring, but there was also an emotional side to this we hadn't anticipated. We hadn't had a chance to take it all in. We'd been on the go for months, and the stillness that night—in a print shop, of all places—made us stop and reflect on how far we had come. In a few hours, we would be walking into uncharted territory, and it was overwhelming, and exhilarating too.

Pulling up to the store that morning was amazing. I saw my name on a beautiful, bright sign (which we had reordered after the first disaster): "Susansnaps: They're Love at First Bite." Inside, as I flipped on the light switch, I was impressed by everything we had accomplished. Mom and I had painted crisp black-and-white stripes on the walls, gray-on-gray polka-dots on the floor, and a vibrant, cheery red on the molding. We'd moved my grand-parents' baking table with the butcher-block top into the center of the store to serve as our counter for our cash register. For the front, we'd collected vintage furniture, china cabinets, and dining tables from flea markets and painted them in shiny white lacquer, to give the shop the feel of an old-fashioned bakery. We'd built a scalloped frame around the front window and matching scalloped shelves, which were neatly lined with bags, boxes, and sparkling glass jars of gingersnaps. As a finishing touch, I'd surprised Mom with a little framed picture of Aunt Sue. I loved our shop, and I believed our customers were going to love it too.

For our opening, we were introducing two new flavors: pnuttysnaps and alohasnaps. Peanut butter cookies are perennially popular, so that prompted us to make peanut butter gingersnaps, and Mom and I like coconut, so we decided to try toasted coconut gingersnaps too. Plus, now I could say my corny line: "A tropical vacation for your taste buds!"

We'd also designed more packaging options, so that there would be something for everybody who came into our store. We had Baby Betty collections in blue and pink, a wedding display, a Holiday Holly theme with Christmas decorations, and more—as many different products as we could dream up.

It was almost ten o'clock. Mom had turned on music, and Frank Sinatra's "My Way" was playing as the oven hummed in the background. The aroma of spices began filling the shop. Our sample tray loaded with five flavors of gourmet gingersnaps was in place.

As I turned our sign to Open, I said, "Mom, are you ready? This is it!"

"Let's make it a good day!" Mom said. She never said, *Have a good day.* It was always up to us whether we would make it a good one or not.

Five minutes later, a woman walked into the shop. "I've been waiting for you to open!" she said. "Wow, your shop is adorable. Okay, let's see—I need fifteen gift boxes in the holiday packaging."

Not bad for our first customer in our new space! The more we heard things like, "You can't," and "That might be hard to do," the more Mom and I told ourselves, "We can." We were open for business.

Dear Sue,

Our phone calls from years ago were still paying off. You and I would have so much fun hashing out paint colors, wallpaper, and furniture for our first homes. That was just another thing we had in common. It's kind of funny, because Susan and I have that in common too.

Through the years, Ken and I have renovated multiple houses. When Susan and I decided to open a new retail shop, I was thrilled that some of what I'd learned would come in handy for the build-out. It was great that Susan was our in-house authority on how to market our cookie business, but I felt good being able to navigate some of the renovation challenges with the confidence of knowing how our efforts would pay off.

And Sue, Susan gave me a wonderful surprise. She put up a framed picture of you in our new shop. It was the first thing I saw when I walked in the morning we opened the store. Susan couldn't have been more thoughtful. It was the photo from your high school graduation. I was fourteen at the time, and you'd given me a copy that I carried around in my wallet just in case I wanted to show off my pretty and "neat" older sister. It has a well-worn crease through the middle from being folded and unfolded countless times.

18

Caller ID

I'VE HAD A FEW PHONE CALLS THAT HAVE CHANGED my life. That's the funny thing about the phone: each time it rings, I never know what I'm going to hear on the other end. Will it be my sister, calling in a panic from a changing room because she's stuck in a dress with a broken zipper? Or my dentist's receptionist, hunting me down for the dreaded dental cleaning that I could swear I just did two weeks ago? Or maybe it will be our family doctor, calling after hours: "Susan, are your parents home? Can you put one of them on the phone?" There is always that split second between hearing the phone ring and answering it, when I think, *What's this going to be?*

Mom and I were having an ordinary day at the store. I was sitting at the desk printing shipping labels while she was packing orders. When the phone rang, I checked the caller ID, like I always did. I would screen our calls, announce whoever was calling, and then pass the phone off to Mom. This time, I called out, "It's New York, New York." I grabbed the phone and held it out to her, but she shook her head. "Mom, take the phone," I urged.

"No," she said. "I'm not going to take it. It's that woman. You know it's her. She's calling back again."

Earlier, Mom had taken a call from a woman in Manhattan who insisted that we had misplaced her order. While Mom used her best diplomacy to convince the disgruntled woman that we would make it right, she frantically wrote the order number on a piece of scratch paper and mouthed, "Look—this—up." I tracked the order, and it was in the woman's building. Mom carefully explained to her that the concierge must have had her package all along.

The phone was still ringing, so I finally gave in and said to Mom, "Okay! I got it." Then, as she went out front, I answered, "Thank you for calling Susansnaps."

On the other end of the line, an upbeat woman said, "Hi! Are you Susan?"

I was thinking, *I don't know, do I want to be?* Hesitantly, I answered, "Yes..."

"Hi! I'm Lauren—a producer from the *CBS Evening News with Katie Couric*. Is now a good time to talk? May I ask you a few questions?"

As I uttered, "Now is perfect," I was simultaneously telling myself, *Don't blow this.* I had sent a letter to CBS, but now I couldn't remember which angle I had taken: delicious cookies, boutique bakery, mother-daughter entrepreneurs, or family with cancer? My mind was racing as I scrolled through my mental Rolodex of letters.

Lauren said, "I work on a segment called 'The American Spirit,' and I came across your video on Daryn Kagan's site. I also went to your website and saw that you have a foundation for cancer patients. I wanted to call and talk to you."

She asked me about all kinds of things—my cancer, how Dad was doing, details about Susansnaps, and how Mom and I work together. I told her about how, as Susansnaps had grown, Mom and I had decided to start a foundation in Aunt Sue's memory that would enable us to donate cookies as gifts to cancer patients. Her questions went on for about fifteen minutes before she landed on the one I'd been listening for. "Sure," I said, my heart racing. "We're free any Monday in October."

I hung up the phone, trembling with excitement, and rushed out into the shop. "Mom, you will not believe this!"

"What is it? Is everything okay?"

Still in disbelief, I said, "That was a producer from the *CBS Evening News with Katie Couric.* They're coming here, Mom. Here—to our shop!"

"Are you kidding? What'd she say?"

Deciphering the notes I'd scribbled, I rattled off, "It's a segment called 'The American Spirit.' We need to have dough ready to bake, the oven going, and a few customers lined up, and they want to film us boxing shipments. We also have to pull together some old photos to help tell our story."

"That's all doable. We're going to be fine."

"Okay." I paused. "But they want something else too."

Mom looked at me. "What's the matter?"

"Lauren said that they want to go with us when we make one of our foundation deliveries."

"They want to go with us to the treatment center? The hospital?"

"Yes. They'll only come here if they can follow us when we deliver Susansnaps, and they want to film me interacting with a few patients. So, we can call Saint Joe's and ask them, but I don't know if we want to agree to this."

What was I afraid of? We had been delivering cookies to local hospitals and treatment centers for years. But we never stayed longer than a couple of minutes. I'd call the day before and make arrangements with the front desk or the head nurse, then Mom would keep the car running as I essentially dashed in and left shopping bags full of cookie gifts for the nurses to share with their patients. It was a quiet, unassuming gesture, and we never wanted to make a big deal out of it.

Of course, I wanted our business to be featured on national television, but I wasn't sure if I was okay with having cameras film us delivering Susansnaps to the hospital. I worried that the segment would come off the wrong way. What if it looked like

Mom and I were exploiting terribly sick patients, just to sell some cookies? Or what if we came off as self-congratulatory? Most of all, I was concerned that the patients would feel uncomfortable with cameras around.

When I was sick, I would not have wanted footage of me to be shown on TV. I probably wouldn't have said anything, but if I had seen a cameraman and a reporter headed my way when I was having chemo, I would've shot Mom a look, and she would've put a stop to it immediately.

Knowing that Katie Couric's team wouldn't come unless we interacted with the patients weighed heavily on me. But the more I thought about it, the more I realized that maybe there was something else making me uncomfortable—more than just worrying about our company's image and the well-being of the patients. The cancer patients I had met were all pretty amazing and could handle just about anything. Perhaps what I was really worrying about was Mom and me.

What would the cameras capture? What if Mom or I got caught off guard? What if it brought back painful memories? It wasn't like we were unaffected by visiting hospitals and cancer centers—it was always emotional. Having cameras with us could be overwhelming.

As much as I wanted the exposure for Susansnaps, I just wasn't sure that a two-and-a-half-minute segment would be worth it.

.... ❧ ....

The day before the *CBS Evening News* team was scheduled to visit, Mom and I worked into the night, making sure everything at the shop was in its place. We washed the windows, mopped the floor, dusted the shelves, restocked the display cases, and made dough.

The next morning, I knew our shop was ready for CBS, but I wasn't so sure that we were ready. We were both too anxious to sit still. Mom was rummaging through her purse for lipstick, and I was fidgeting with a tape dispenser. "So, Suz," Mom said, "what do you think they're going to ask us?"

"What do you mean?" I asked. "Mom, they're going to watch us bake and film the shop. We're just supposed to do what we do every day."

"Susan, you know they're coming for more than that. They'll want us to talk about how we got started. Do you think we should practice?"

I knew Mom was right—we were about to go on national TV, after all. But I didn't want the two of us to sit there rehashing our life story two minutes before the film crew showed up. "Mom, don't worry. We'll be good."

Just then, an oversize black SUV pulled up outside. As two men headed toward the door, Mom took the opportunity to say, "Susan, whatever happens, this is incredible."

Mom chatted with the crew as they unpacked their equipment, but I hung back, wondering how the day was going to unfold. Suddenly, the front door flew open and in blew this tiny ball of energy—Lauren.

She took in the shop in one glance. "This is beautiful! This is going to be good!"

Lauren continued to buzz around the room while Mom and I tried to play it cool as we clipped sound packs to the back of our pants, pulled the wires up our shirts, and stuck tiny microphones onto our aprons. Once we were all hooked up and the cameraman and sound guy were in place, we went into motion. Mom cranked dough through our cookie drop and I sprinkled sugar on top of each gingersnap. So far so good—the baking was under control. But it was dead silent in the shop. I could practically hear the sugar bouncing off the cookie sheets. Breaking the uncomfortable silence, the cameraman startled me by saying, "Do you two ever talk to each other?"

"Oh, yes!" I said. "We talk nonstop. We didn't know we were supposed to."

"Don't pay attention to us. Pretend like we're not even here. Do what you normally do."

Well, that was all Mom and I needed to hear. I started thinking about the suit that Barbara Walters had worn on her show the day before, and the first thing that came out of my mouth was, "Did you see *The View* yesterday?"

Mom didn't say anything, so I looked up from sugaring the gingersnaps. We always talked about *The View*; it was one of our favorite shows. I wondered, *What's the problem?*

"Sweetie," she said, a tight smile on her face, "what did you make for dinner last night?" Then it hit me. *The View* with Barbara Walters was a show on ABC. We were filming for CBS and Katie Couric. The guy with the earpiece listening to our every word, the cameraman zooming in on our faces, and the producer taking notes were all from CBS. I ducked my head and murmured something about making spaghetti. After that, I made sure to keep the rest of our conversation away from anything TV-related!

While we were baking cookies, the reporter, Mark, arrived. I could see him typing notes on his BlackBerry as he took in each detail.

By eleven thirty, after just two hours, we'd finished taking Mark and the crew through "a day in the life of Laura and Susan at work," and we were on our way to the hospital. The twenty-minute car ride was a welcome reprieve, since Mom and I drove in our car while the film crew followed behind us.

Mom and I started talking so fast that we were talking over each other. "How do you think it's going?" I asked.

"I think Lauren's nice. The guys are fine. They obviously know what they're doing—they're pros. And the reporter—wasn't it funny that Mark said that when he told his wife, 'I'm going to Susansnaps today,' she told him all about us?"

Just as she finished her sentence, I threw my hand over the microphone attached to my apron. "Mom!" I whispered. "Mom... Mom!" When I got her attention, I pointed to her mic. "These are still on!" It was embarrassing but funny, and it made for a good distraction.

When we reached the hospital's parking deck, Mom pushed the intercom. "We're here for oncology radiation," she called out. We'd been there many times, so this was all familiar, but the next thing I knew, Mom was driving up the exit lane. It was bad enough we went the wrong way, but we had the crew following behind us in their SUV too. I guess Mom must've been feeling as nervous as I was.

Ever since we'd agreed to do this, I'd been trying to prepare myself by envisioning our visit to the radiation and chemo center. I sometimes had flashbacks to my treatment that always seemed to happen at the most random and inopportune times. One whiff of a very precise scent, and I'd be right back in the infusion center. One bite of something slightly metallic-tasting, and all I'd think of would be the wretched taste of chemicals running through my veins. I didn't want to have a "moment" while cameras were capturing my every move at the center. So I figured if I envisioned the day and planned for the worst, I could build up some kind of immunity to my own memories, and everything would go smoothly.

As Mom and I approached the entrance to the hospital, the

cameras were already rolling. This was nuts. For all the times Mom had propped me up so I could shuffle through these sliding doors, I never thought the two of us would be returning here with one of the largest news stations in the country covering our story. We'd barely made it through the door before we walked straight into an unexpected meet and greet with hospital administrators and their marketing team. Some of them were shaking hands with Mom and hugging me, while others were vying for time in front of the camera. Our entourage kept growing, and the attention was making me uncomfortable. The last thing I wanted was to make any of the patients in the waiting room uneasy, but they could already see chaos brewing on the other side of the glass wall. What normally would have been a low-key cookie drop-off had evolved into staged news coverage of us and a PR opportunity for the hospital.

Noticing that my mom and I had stepped aside and were having a private conference, the cameraman approached us. "Ladies, is everything okay?"

Mom said, "This is not how Susan and I do this."

He leaned toward me reassuringly, with the camera on his shoulder. "Don't worry about us. Do what you feel comfortable doing. I'll follow you."

My heart was thumping as I made my way to the front desk and asked for the head nurse. When she came around the corner to greet me, her eyes immediately got misty. Mine did too. "Susan, look at you!" she said. "You look great... How ya feeling? Having you come back means so much to us, and the patients love the cookies." Unfortunately, the producer wanted a different camera angle, so we had to reenact the greeting, which was awkward.

Then we started handing out cookies to the patients. Mom and I were being rushed around the radiation waiting room so fast there wasn't a chance to say more than a few words to anyone. It wasn't clear to me what Mom and I were supposed to be doing, and it felt uncomfortable. As we were about to go back out to the lobby, Mom tapped my shoulder. "Susan, there's a woman who would like to speak with you."

The woman, who was there for treatment, asked me, "Are you one of the crew? Or are you one of us?"

I said, "I'm one of you," and her face lit up. She was excited to find that we had something in common: cancer.

Before I walked away, my new friend—a very elderly African American woman—looked up from her wheelchair, smiling, and said, "I sure hope one day I look exactly like you." I wanted her to look like me too, and I knew that neither of us were talking about being young and blond.

Without missing a beat, I smiled right back and said, "You will!"

Hearing that, the woman's daughter, and everyone else in the room, broke into laughter. While the camera might have captured me doing a good deed by visiting an ill woman, she was the one who had done me a favor.

Leaving the radiation center, I felt at ease. As we headed to the elevators to go up to the chemo center, Mom put her arm around me and gave me a reassuring squeeze. "Good job, sweetie."

Catching up with the crew, we stuffed ourselves and the equipment into the elevator. Riding up, I reminded myself, *Once the visit to the chemo floor is over, we'll get back to happy cookies, happy store, happy us.*

Stepping off the elevator, Mom pointed Lauren in the direction of the chemo center while the rest of us held back and waited for the go-ahead. Hanging out with Mark and the crew, I couldn't resist asking them a series of questions. I was intrigued by their work, but I also wanted to shift the conversation away from me. We began talking about past stories they'd covered, places they'd traveled, things they'd seen. As Mom joined us and they continued bantering, a voice in my head screamed, *You're trying, but I won't let you forget where you are.* Pushing that away, I smiled and nodded like I was still in the conversation, but I felt myself slipping. I was thinking too much.

Mom glanced over. "Hon, are you okay? You're white as a sheet."

I turned my head away from the group, hoping that it would help me hold it together, but it actually made things worse. My eyes landed on the waiting room at the end of the long hallway, and my thoughts went back to a different time. I went back to the day that I sat innocently in that waiting room, flanked by Mom and Dad, before my bone marrow biopsy—a test that would tell us whether my cancer had spread. Although that test had happened years ago, it felt like yesterday, and I was sad thinking about that twenty-two-year-old girl. She had no idea what was ahead of her or how bad things would get.

On the day of the test, I wanted to be brave. I worked at convincing myself, *I can do this alone. It really can't be that bad.* Dad joined us for that appointment. Selfishly, I was glad he was there for me; but more than that, I was relieved he could keep Mom company. Even so, their dual presence wasn't very calming. Dad kept his head down and his elbows on his knees, and his left leg bounced steadily while he rubbed his hands back and forth. Mom talked incessantly about where I wanted to eat after the test. I wanted to show them both that I had things under control.

Unfortunately, all three of us were acutely aware of how brutal this test could be and the gravity of its results. Mom had told me, "Aunt Sue said it felt like she'd been shot by a rifle," and Dad said the pain during his test was so excruciating that he passed out. As a kid, I loved hearing stories about my invincible aunt, but right then, I wished Mom hadn't shared that particular memory of her sister. As the minutes ticked by, I compartmentalized, thinking, *That was them, and that was then. This is me, right now.*

When I heard a nurse call, "Susan Stachler," I jumped up

and, using anger to mask my growing fear, I firmly told my parents to stay where they were. I actually said to them, "I don't need you."

I was so unprepared for what I saw when I turned the corner. I should have kept my head down as I followed the nurse, but it was too late. I was faced with one vast room of sickness: a menagerie of hospital beds, machines beeping, tubes dripping, clear bags filled with God knows what, and that smell. As we wove our way past frighteningly ill patients to the private room in the back, it seemed like everything around me was happening in slow motion. With each step, I felt increasingly shocked. *What is this place? Aunt Sue did this? How did Dad make this seem okay?* I was scared.

Grateful that the gregarious nurse was a pro at mixing mindless conversation with details of the upcoming procedure, I politely answered her questions. I thought things were going well, until I saw a look of sympathy come across the seasoned nurse's face. As I watched the second hand on the wall clock tick, I knew time was running out before Dr. Weens would arrive to perform the test. The third time the nurse asked, "Honey, are you *sure* you don't want your parents?" my confidence was replaced by utter vulnerability.

Discouraged, I said, "I'm sorry, but do you think you could get my mom?" There was no way I was going to let Dad relive this.

I was already lying flat on my stomach on the examination table when Mom entered and moved her chair up so she could place her face next to mine. As Dr. Weens began prepping me with a series of numbing needle punctures, I clutched Mom's hand with a fearful grip. Eyes closed as I braced for what was still to come, I listened to Mom repeating, "Look at me, Susan. Keep breathing." My tiny doctor stood on a stool for leverage and jabbed a large tubular needle into the top ridge of my back hip bone. I screamed, a high, piercing shriek.

I shook my head, pulling myself back to the present, and froze when I looked over and saw the camera. It wasn't on, but I thought, *If I fall apart, that's the footage they'll use.* I was not going to let this segment become "Former Patient Breaks Down on Return to Hospital."

Mom touched my arm, repeating, "Hon, are you okay?"

"I don't think so," I answered quietly. The room was beginning to spin, and I could feel tears coming. I needed to step away.

As Mom assured the guys, "We'll be right back," I ducked into a nearby bathroom.

Letting the cool water run over my wrists, I kept my head down and focused my attention on vigorously washing my hands. Then, leaning on the bathroom counter, I stared straight into the mirror and repeated out loud, "I'm fine. I'm fine." I hoped if I said it enough, I'd shake this. But my eyes were turning puffy and red from holding in tears. *Great—this doesn't look good.*

Mom gave me my space, but gently said, "If you want, we can stop. I'll tell them we're done."

"What?" I said. "No, I don't want that. We're not stopping." I turned around and caught a glimpse of Mom's face. It was evident we were both flooded by memories. "I started thinking about—"

"Pull yourself together," Mom said abruptly, cutting me off.

It was out of character for her to be so sharp with me, but that was exactly what I needed to hear. I took a deep breath, and we walked back out. Before anyone could ask, Mom announced, "We're all good. Where do you want us?"

Lauren called out, "We need them coming down the hallway, side by side."

Mom and I each picked up two oversize shopping bags, and the camera crew told us to stand shoulder to shoulder and walk casually down the hallway.

I quickly said, "Pssst…Mom, where are you going to look?"

"Look at me, and we'll pretend we are talking to each other."

"I think I might smile. Should we?"

We started down the hallway squished side by side, only making it halfway before we burst out laughing. Apparently we looked as ridiculous as we felt because we had the crew laughing with us. We ended up having to walk up and down the hallway several times before they got the shot they wanted—so much for being natural!

Once they were finished with that shot, Mark approached my mom. "Laura, can I ask? What happened out there?" I was standing across the room, and I think he assumed that I couldn't hear him.

"Mark, I don't know if anyone told you, but Susan was a patient here," Mom said.

Out of the corner of my eye, I saw Mark nod to the cameraman as he moved up beside me. "What's it like being back here, Susan?" Cautiously, he began asking me a series of questions as the camera pulled within ten inches of my face and the boom mic dangled above my head.

I realized he wanted me to say something meaningful. Mark was questioning me as a survivor, as some sort of authority on cancer. I had never thought of myself that way before, so I didn't have a canned answer. "It's nice to come back," I said. "Sometimes it's hard though. Treatment was rough. But I'm okay. I feel lucky." Then I looked down at the shopping bags in my hand and said, "We're just delivering cookies. We have sixty small gifts. We hope they will bring sixty smiles."

Mark nodded and seemed satisfied with my response. "So what about earlier?" Mark asked. "What were you thinking?"

Before I could begin to try to explain what it felt like to come back here and think about Mom, Dad, and Aunt Sue and how we were all linked by this disease, a nurse interrupted. "Susan, we're all set."

As the nurse guided Mom and me from patient to patient to hand out cookies, the crew followed respectfully behind us, and my worries about exploitation went out the window. We passed out bags of gingersnaps and met some very nice people, and I got into an engaging conversation with one man about our mutual love of cheeseburgers, especially ones with extra cheese. As we went into specific detail on our favorite toppings, the man's oxygen mask, tubes, IVs, hospital gown, skeletal frame, and frailty faded away. He was just a guy who liked a good meal. As I listened to him share his medical history along with his opinions on the ideal burger, I worried that this lovely, spunky man might never eat another one.

In the end, the film crew captured the patients exactly as I'd hoped they would: as people who happened to be sick, not *sick people*.

As we started to leave, the floor oncologist approached us. "It's a pleasure to meet you," she said to me. "I was just informed that you have been treated here at St. Joe's?"

"Yes," I said.

"No one ever comes back here," she told me. "This is a forgotten wing. I can't believe you brought a news crew with you to share what goes on here. Thank you for remembering my patients." Her comments almost left Mom and me speechless. I was grateful she took the time to speak with us. By the time we left, Mom and I thought the visit went nicely.

Now all that was left to do was return to the store for a final interview. Back at the shop, the crew rearranged our entire setup to make it easier to shoot, sliding our seven-foot cookie racks around the kitchen, pushing our steel baking tables back, and setting up their equipment. The producer and crew took their respective places around the cameras and monitors as they put in their earpieces. Someone shut off the store's overhead fluorescent lights, and we sat in the dark until they turned on their ultrabright interview lights. Blinded by the spotlights beaming directly on our faces, we could barely see Mark.

While the lights were being adjusted, Mark took us through the usual questions about Susansnaps: where the recipe for the gingersnaps had come from, what other flavors we'd tried, how long we'd had the store. Our conversation was rolling along easily when I saw the little red recording light flip on. Suddenly, Mark's demeanor went from informal to professional. "Tell me how all this started."

Mom had our elevator speech down pat, so she began with her routine spiel. When she was finished, Mark asked, "Laura, you said it was *your* husband, *your* daughter, and *your* sister, right? All three had cancer?"

Smiling, Mom said matter-of-factly, "Yes, that's correct."

He nodded. "Was that hard for you?"

"No. I am so proud of them."

I wasn't sure that Mark was buying her cheery facade, as he simply responded, "I'm sure you are."

Mom was giving quick, confident answers, but I thought

she might be coming across as a bit emotionless. She was smiling as she said things like, "Yes, my sister died at twenty-eight, and my husband was diagnosed at forty-one with incurable cancer."

The interview was taking longer than I'd expected. I began to get a little sweaty, and trying to sit up super straight was making my back stiff. Mark kept asking questions, so he clearly hadn't gotten what he was looking for yet.

Mark asked again, "Laura, your husband and daughter had chemo side by side. What were you thinking?"

Quietly, Mom said, "I was thinking, 'First my husband, now my child—it's too much. I can't do it.'"

What? I thought. *Oh no.* All this time, Mom had remained completely stoic. She had never once said out loud how hard it had been for her. I knew that it was, of course, but hearing her say it out loud, I was surprised and touched.

Then Mark asked, "Did it make you think of your sister? Can you tell me about her? What was your sister like?"

I was supposed to sit facing the cameras, but I couldn't any longer. I heard an unfamiliar quiver in Mom's voice. I glanced over at her and saw her stricken face. I could see she was lost in thought, back on the hillside at Queen of Heaven Cemetery in California, saying goodbye to her sister. I started talking, attempting to turn the attention away from Mom. "She was so creative," I began, repeating a story Mom had told me about Aunt Sue, Christmas presents, her elaborate wrapping, and her love for gifting. *What am I saying?* I thought. But at least I was making Aunt Sue sound real.

My story wasn't going anywhere, but Mark listened graciously. We bantered back and forth as I shared what Aunt Sue was like and how proud she would be of Mom. For that one second, I was happy those words had rolled off my tongue. I was glad Mom had heard me say that out loud.

"Susan, you were named for your aunt?" Mark asked.

"Yes, that's right. My parents named me after her."

"You both had Hodgkin's and were treated at the same age?"

"Yes, we both did chemo and radiation at twenty-two."

"Did you ever meet her?"

I shook my head. "I feel like I know her, but no, we never met. She died before I was born."

He nodded. "She died as a result of Hodgkin's lymphoma?"

"Yes."

"Your Aunt Susan died from the same disease that you were diagnosed with?"

The room fell silent. The producer and crew, who had been watching monitors and focusing on their responsibilities, looked up at me now and seemed to be hanging on my every word.

"Susan?" Mark prompted.

I thought I knew where he was going with this, but he was too nice to actually say it. I gripped the side of my stool and leaned forward. "Are you asking me if I thought I was going to die?"

Dear Sue,

I didn't sleep at all that night. I'd had the standard interview questions down pat, but I couldn't stop thinking about how I'd frozen up when Mark asked about you. Over and over, I heard my response, the empty adjectives that I'd used: "sweet" and "kind" and "nice." I was heartbroken. That's not how I feel about you.

Susan is the only one who knows what happened the next morning. We went through our usual routine of opening the shop. Both of us were tired from the day before, and neither of us were talking. For once, I didn't want to chat. I knew that, eventually, Susan would ask me how I thought the interview had gone.

I was feeling awful, but I didn't want to let on. I told her that I thought it went well and that she did a beautiful job. We continued to go over every detail of the day, and Susan said, "Mark is really good at what he does." I had to agree with her. Drained, I went to sit down at the empty shipping table. Susan asked me what was wrong, but I didn't want to tell her what I was thinking.

I was upset because I'd done a bad job. That's how I felt. I was aching inside. I'd wanted to tell Mark that not a day goes by that I don't miss you, and that I love you. But I couldn't. And I don't know why. Why was that so hard? As soon as he asked about you, I got lost in my own thoughts. In my mind, I *was seeing your casket at the cemetery. And then suddenly, on the flip side, I was sitting in our shop, next to Susan, with a reporter who was asking about you. I wanted to say that you were amazing, that you were the most amazing person ever, and that I am better for having known you. I am better because you lived. But instead, I just kept saying that you were nice. You were! But that wasn't enough. It wasn't nearly enough to show people how much you meant to me and how much I still miss you.*

"Mom, what's the matter?" Susan asked again.

I tried to brush her question off and change the topic, but Susan knows me too well. She could tell something was bothering me. Finally, I admitted, "I just don't think I did very well."

Susan feigned surprise, but we both knew what I was talking about.

"I did a bad job," I said. "I didn't answer Mark's questions. You know. When he asked about Aunt Sue." I could feel myself coming undone.

Susan responded softly, "You did answer him, Mom. I know they'll put the piece together nicely."

I knew she was right, but I didn't care about what Mark and his crew thought. And no matter what Susan said to try to convince me otherwise, I felt terrible.

"I didn't get her right," I insisted. "You know that. I had my chance, and I failed."

Susan started getting upset. "That's not true. You told him how nice Aunt Sue was."

"No, you know I didn't," I said, starting to cry. "I had a chance to tell everyone how wonderful she was, how strong and brave she was. I wanted to say how much I loved her, how she was my hero."

"Mom, stop," Susan said. "Don't say that. Look at all you've done."

"No!" I said, my voice rising. "I failed her. Nobody will ever know her now!"

The shop was silent. Finally, Susan said quietly, "I do, Mom. I know Aunt Sue. I know her."

I was stunned. I stopped and looked up at Susan. She was right. She does know you in a unique way that I never will. I'm not sure if it's possible to be both comforted and profoundly sad at the same time, but I was.

19

A Round
of Margaritas

I LOVE MEXICAN FOOD. IT'S DELICIOUS, AND I THINK
of it as fun, festive, happy food. It might sound funny, but every
time I have Mexican food, I feel like it's a personal fiesta, a miniature celebration of life. Who knew that going out to grab chips
and salsa, tacos, and a margarita could mean so much? But to me,
and to Mom, it does.

Thanksgiving had come and gone. It was November 30,
2010. Only twenty-five days remained until Christmas, and while
the economy still wasn't that great and a lot of companies were
cutting back, we were fortunate to have not only personal orders
coming in, but also a handful of important corporate orders. Our
calendar was filling up: we had to ship 250 gift tins one day, get
400 bakery bags ready for pickup the next, prepare 96 gift sets for
a company party, assemble 24 cases for a gift-basket business, and

so on. But beyond those set orders, we weren't expecting much else to come up. We decorated the store with Christmas trees, ornaments, elves, candy canes, artificial snow, and giant presents that we hung from the ceiling. It looked magical. Mom and I made it enchanting. We played Bing Crosby's "White Christmas" and the soundtrack from *A Charlie Brown Christmas*, one of my favorites. The oven was busy, and it smelled like Santa's bakeshop.

Our piece with CBS had not aired yet, and each day that passed, I figured our chances were growing smaller and smaller. We'd been bumped a few times, and each time we were taken off the schedule, I thought that it might never happen. *CBS Evening News* covers breaking news and major headlines, so we understood that our cookie story might take a back seat. Still, it was beginning to stress me out, all the waiting, the not hearing, the wondering. I checked in with Lauren once or twice, but all she would say was, "I'll let you know." Mom and I knew we couldn't keep worrying about something that was out of our control, so we focused on filling the orders we had.

Around four o'clock that afternoon, Lauren called. "Hi, Susan. The piece is airing tonight. Can't wait for you to see it."

She sounded busy, so I calmly replied, "This is great! We're excited to see how it came together. Thank you for letting us know." What I wanted to say was, *Wait—what? Tonight? Like, in less than three hours? No way!* But I kept that thought to myself. Or at least, I did for as long as it took me to hang up the phone.

"We're on tonight!" I said to Mom, grinning from ear to ear.

We started talking a mile a minute, wondering everything from, "Did we sound okay?" and "What do you think the store will look like?" to "Where should we go to celebrate?" We were going to be on TV, so no matter what happened, we were at least going to toast ourselves. Before leaving, we told our friends and family that our spot was going to be on the evening news that night.

Then Mom and I locked up the store and went home—Mom to her house, me to the one I now shared with Randy. You'd think we would've watched it together, but we were too nervous. Millions of people were about to see what we do on TV. I met up with Randy at home and paced back and forth in my living room when the opening shot of our store came onto the screen.

I heard the familiar hum of our oven and the rhythmic clanking of our cookie machine coming through my flat-screen TV. Mark's eloquent, professional voice said, "Laura Stachler and her daughter Susan built a gourmet cookie business one sheet of gingersnaps at a time." My thoughts were racing as the brief piece continued. The cookies looked good, the store looked bright and happy, and Mom and I looked okay. *Phew.* Mark made us sound like the company we wanted to be. They showed a picture of my family. Then one of Aunt Sue. I couldn't believe my eyes. The hospital shots looked great, which I was relieved to see. Mark ended with, "Proud of every Susansnap's secret ingredient: kindness."

A little while later, Mom, Dad, Randy, and I met up at a local Mexican restaurant. We ordered guacamole and a round of margaritas, then went on to rehash the piece and share funny stories and memories of everything and anything that had gone on over the past few years. Dad interjected, "That was great. You both were really great."

Mom raised her glass. "To Sue. And thanks to you, sweetie, millions of people tonight know her. Incredible."

Aunt Sue's story is part of my story; it took me a while to wrap my head around that.

Suddenly, Mom said, "I wonder if we'll get much of a response?"

I replied, "If you want to check, pull out your phone."

She got out her phone and looked down at the screen. "Susan! Look at your phone. Is this right?"

I leaned over. "Oh my gosh. Those are orders."

"I know. Grab your phone and take a look."

I opened up my email inbox and watched the messages flooding in. "Sixty-four. Wait! Sixty-seven!"

Mom said, "No. I'm seeing seventy-two."

Our inbox was inundated with order notifications, emails from viewers, and people signing up for our email list. Within twenty-four hours, we had eight hundred online orders. And they kept coming for weeks: holiday orders, get-well gifts, thinking-of-you gifts, and corporate orders. Some customers said they'd ordered because "The cookies looked good," but many more people told us, "We just love what you do!" The phone was ringing nonstop. Finally, it felt like we had taken this crazy little cookie idea of ours and really started to make a difference.

.... ❧ ....

The next few weeks were insane; as the orders poured in, we became crazy busy. There was no time to stop and train anyone new or reorganize the way we were doing things. We just had to hit the ground running and keep going. It was like we were a snake swallowing a mouse. We had a big blob of orders, totaling thousands of items that all needed to be shipped within a few days, and we were simultaneously dealing with our existing, and increasing, holiday business. The phone was ringing nonstop. We'd answer a call and take an order, only to hang up and have four new messages waiting.

People were flocking to the store in droves. Maybe we should've locked the door for a day to regroup and map out a plan of attack, but we didn't. We had family and some close friends pitching in when they could, but at the end of the day, it came down to the two of us. No one was going to care the same way we did. It got so bad that Mom and I didn't even have time to do laundry, and my friend Stephanie had to go shopping to get new clothes for us. Mom had to call UPS and schedule double pickups. The truck would come once in the morning and then again at our regular time, between four and five o'clock every afternoon. Every time someone asked for an item we'd run out of, I wanted to cry.

But we had dreamed of this kind of success, and we were not going to fail. Each order, each customer, each comment, each email, each phone call, each dollar was important to us. But we certainly learned that being successful is not always easy, and things don't always go smoothly. One big issue was a glitch in the settings on our website. Because the box for automation wasn't checked on the order page, we had to process every online order manually. That meant printing out every order, entering the credit card information by hand, and inputting the information for the shipping label. And our online store was inundated with traffic. The system had worked fine when we had eight, twelve, or even twenty orders a day, but it became incredibly time-consuming when hundreds of orders were coming in—and we didn't have any time to spare! We stayed in constant motion for more than three weeks straight. At one point, Mom was so tired that she would take a shower, get dressed for work the next day, and lie down on the couch, afraid that if she got into bed, she'd never wake up!

About five days into this crazy period, I looked at Mom and, amid the chaos around us, said decisively, "We are not failing at this."

She agreed. Although we were being bombarded with an outpouring of support and interest from all these new customers, part of me felt like we had choked. I think our exhaustion made us feel like we weren't going to pull this off. And the more that idea crept in, the more I thought, *Do we know what we're doing?* Luckily, that fear only fueled us to push harder and plow ahead. That, and the response we were getting from our customers, which was truly inspiring. Cancer patients would email and say, "Your cookies are the only thing I can eat!" We were getting dozens of calls and emails from people just thanking us for doing something good and urging us to keep going. It was amazing. And it was clear we were doing something more important than just baking cookies—we were making people happy.

So even though we would work until one or two o'clock in the morning and be back at it by five, it was worth it. And the more my hands ached and my feet throbbed, the more I would think, *I am lucky!* During our busiest days, I would stop and say to myself, *I am blessed to be here, doing exactly this.* And, somehow, we just kept going.

One day, we had to bake fourteen thousand gingersnaps, in all five flavors, which was really a no-no for us. It created a logistical challenge, and we had to box cookies as fast as we could to avoid a clutter of different flavors piling up. Throughout the day, our seasonal bakers would toss any irregularly sized or shaped cookies, of any flavor, into sample bags that our helpers could take home. The rejects were still delicious, after all.

As Bobby, one of our guys who helped with packaging and

shipping, was finishing up for the day, I said, "Don't forget your sample bag." A minute later, when I saw him going from table to table, I asked, "Hey, what's wrong?"

"My bag was right here..." he answered.

"Okay. Right where? Where is it now?"

His eyes got as big as saucers, and he started laughing nervously. "Oh no."

"Bobby! Did you box it up and ship it?" I asked, already knowing that he had.

I don't like mistakes, and I've been known to get feisty when it comes to wanting things done right. But this was too funny to be mad about. Our shipments had already been picked up for the day; his sample bag was long gone. Someone in America got a really special treat. We waited for a customer to call complaining about it, but apparently the recipient enjoyed their assortment, because we never heard anything.

Somehow, we survived the glorious mayhem. In the end, all the orders that needed to be delivered by the holidays made it.

We'd had our most epic holiday season to date. But even if we hadn't, we still would've celebrated. That's what we do. Whether we've had sales or no sales, big orders or small orders, a profitable year or a year where we're barely hanging on, we've always—since the very first holiday season that I started helping Mom—marked a year of work at our favorite Mexican restaurant, Nuevo Laredo Cantina. This December, during our super long workdays, you'd hear us calling out, "What are you going to order at Nuevo?" or "What do you think, tacos or enchiladas?"

Mexican food has a special place in our family that goes back to when Aunt Sue was in treatment. After finishing a horrible round of chemo that had required her to be hospitalized for days, Aunt Sue insisted that her husband take her out for Mexican, so she could celebrate with a margarita. The image of my young aunt leaving the hospital, weakened but wanting to go out, wanting to celebrate life, is one that has always stuck with me. I couldn't begin to count how many times I've thought about that story. It has nothing to do with Mexican food, and everything to do with the fact that Aunt Sue created her own happiness, even under the worst circumstances. I'll never drink a margarita without thinking about my aunt.

Before we headed out for that year's dinner, Mom put a note on the front door of the store: "Closed for End of the Year Party. Thank You for Making It a Good Year!" I was sitting at the computer, checking delivery statuses for the last time, while Mom was busy taking post-holiday inventory. It was the first quiet day we'd had in weeks, and I finally had some time to think about everything we'd accomplished. I was surprised to feel my lower lip begin to quiver.

"Mom," I said quietly. "Do you ever think about what it took for us to get here?" I was exhausted, physically and emotionally.

Mom sat down in a chair across from me. "Yes, sweetie, I do."

A few tears streamed down my face. "I love what we do, and I love working here. But you and I own a gingersnap cookie company. *Gingersnaps.* This was never supposed to happen."

Mom nodded. Then she came over and wrapped her arms around me as she whispered in my ear, "I love working with you too."

Dear Sue,

I love answering questions and taking orders at work. It's a good thing, especially after we were on TV. I took more than one hundred phone orders in the first two days. It was crazy! I was floored by how much our two-minute spot had meant to people, and how carefully they had listened to and remembered the details.

I'd answer the phone and hear, "I saw CBS, the show about the mother and daughter who started this cookie company. I wanted to ask how the girl and her dad are doing." I couldn't believe it.

I always thanked the caller for watching and for their thoughtful comments, then proceeded with the business of taking their order.

On one of the first of these calls, when I was nearly ready to hang up, the pleasant woman on the line said, "Wait. I wanted to say something else to you. I just wanted to tell you, I'm really sorry about your sister." That just about took my breath away. She'd seen your picture on TV and remembered your part in Susansnaps.

I have to laugh thinking about how you'd call me from Carver's after a dinner shift and say, "I'm leaving soon, so get the tube warmed up!" It took a few minutes for the TV to come into focus. By the time you got home and walked into my room, we'd be ready to watch The Tonight Show together.

Decades later, I sat in my family room watching television and heard your name, saw a picture of you and me together on the news. We were on TV. Unimaginable.

Sugar Crystals

JANUARY CAME AND, FOR THE FIRST TIME, MOM AND I decided to reward ourselves with a bonus. Coincidentally, around the same time, I stumbled upon some amazing airfare rates on Delta.

"Remember what Lauren from CBS said? Before she left here?" I asked Mom. "She said that we should let her know when we're in town and that we're welcome at CBS anytime."

Mom said, "Yes, why?"

"Well, there are flights to LaGuardia for one hundred twenty-nine dollars. That's practically buy one, get one free. Let's go!"

I didn't have to say much more to convince her.

A few weeks later, we landed in New York and headed over to CBS. Lauren gave us a tour, introducing us around the newsroom and to people who had helped put our piece together. We weren't sure if we would have a chance to meet Katie Couric—she had an incredibly tight schedule. After the tour, Lauren welcomed us to take a seat in her office and said, "Get your camera ready. There are no guarantees, but Katie does have to walk by my office on the way to the studio."

It was like we were waiting for Elvis or something, and I started to feel a little silly. I wanted to say hello, of course, but I didn't want to look like some overeager fan, and I was painfully conscious that everyone there was very busy and we were taking up their time.

Lauren's phone rang. She picked it up, then turned to us. "Katie knows you're here, but she is very busy…"

I was just about to tell her not to worry about it when Katie Couric zoomed by the office, waving to us through the window. We waved back, and then, to my surprise, Katie dashed through the door and gave me a hug.

"Hi! How are you?" she asked, then looked over to Mom. "How is your husband?" Then she said, "I'm sorry. I don't have much time. You're welcome to watch me film."

We followed her into the studio and watched her work. I was still really hoping I would get a minute to say something to her. I didn't know exactly what to say, but I felt the need to let her know how much her support meant to us. I was secretly hoping she'd nail the promos without having to redo them, so that maybe there would be a minute or two to spare in her schedule.

But her assistant had come over to us. "Thank you for coming," she said as she politely shooed us toward the door. My heart sank.

Then Katie called out, "Wait! Do you have a few minutes? Can you come to my office?" I could not believe it.

The assistant looked impressed. "Well, aren't you something? This never happens."

Lady, I know! I thought. *There are a lot of things that weren't supposed to happen but did!*

Mom and I followed Katie up a narrow flight of stairs to her office, and she invited us to sit down on her couch. My head was spinning—all I could think of was how far we had come, from the chemo recliner, to the garage bakeshop, to the store, and now here.

Katie asked how we were doing, and she was genuinely interested in hearing more of our story. Just like that, the three of us began talking. It became a personal visit as we talked about cancer and family. She understood a lot of the stuff we had gone through, and at one point, she even got up and grabbed a framed picture of her family off her desk and showed it to us. She asked about Susansnaps and tossed out names of editors at major magazines who she thought we should contact. Maybe I should have asked her if she could make some introductions or give us their contact information, but, honestly, I was just happy to be sitting there and chatting with her. I was enjoying where I was in that moment. I had learned to appreciate what was in front of me. I was taking it all in. I wish I could say I took this opportunity to say something profound, but the words got stuck somewhere between staring at the Susansnap sugar crystals clinging to Katie's lip gloss and appreciating all it had taken for us to get here. Mom, me, and Susansnaps.

Dear Sue,

There's something I want to tell you. Remember when I was starting out with the dessert business and I asked Susan to help me? I told you I didn't know what I was doing. I didn't back then, but I still coerced Susan into working for me, and I'm so glad she did. Eventually, working side by side, we figured out how to get Susansnaps up and going.

On a regular basis, customers ask me, "Does your daughter still work for you?" When I answer, "No, not anymore," they look perplexed and almost disappointed. I actually kind of enjoy it. In that split second, I always think, What a wild ride this has been! *And I feel my heart swell with pride over Susan. Sue, through the years something changed. Susan has gradually taken the lead on our cookie company. Then, I continue with a smile, "Actually, I work for her now," and before I allow for any reaction, I add, "and it's great!"*

21

Unsnappable

AS MOM AND I RODE IN A TAXI TOWARD ABC'S STUDIO in Times Square, I couldn't help but think of the girl I used to be, that college girl with the black interview suit. The one who liked everything planned and organized. The one who liked to read the last page of a book before she began the first. I'm not convinced she would have shown up for this day. But that girl had changed. Mom and I had changed together. We went after things differently now. This day was a perfect example. It was July of 2015, and we were on our way to meet David Muir, anchor of ABC's *World News Tonight*, who was going to interview us for the show's "Made in America" segment. When we'd received an email from the producer at 1:00 a.m. with our final travel details, informing us that we had to catch a 7:45 a.m. flight, we didn't think twice about it.

On the plane, all I hoped was that my puffy morning face

would go away and my deep, manly morning voice would wear off by the time we arrived in New York. As soon as we landed, we went to baggage claim to meet our driver, as we'd been instructed, but there was no driver to be found. Mom and I split up and searched for a driver with a sign for "Stachler" or "Laura and Susan" or even "Susansnaps." We looked, we looked again, we circled the baggage claim. No one was there.

Then a string of phone calls began with the dispatcher telling us, "Look for a man with glasses in a Hawaiian shirt. He didn't have time to make a sign."

Are they joking? But we didn't question it; we just began looking for the man. We went outside, up and down the sidewalk, until the driver called Mom's phone. He was in gate D. We were in B. He kept saying, "Great. I am in D too," and Mom kept repeating, "B. We are in *bee*. B like *boy*." Time was ticking.

Just then, the producer called and asked, "Are you on your way?"

Remaining composed, Mom responded, "Yes, of course." But we weren't. We weren't even in a moving vehicle.

We should have just flagged down our own taxi, but we thought, *ABC sent a driver, so we should wait.* I'm not sure if I've ever seen Mom more frantic. It was outrageous, but I started laughing. Don't get me wrong, I was panicked too, but Mom already had that covered for both of us, and I didn't know what else to do. I just followed any instructions she barked out at me.

I'm not a runner, and certainly not in public, but when she said, "Run back inside! Look for a Hawaiian shirt," I did.

At one point, Mom spotted a man with glasses and yanked open the door of his van, yelling, "Susan, get in!"

But as I was trying to take a seat, I saw that he was clearly not our driver, since he was waving a sign that said "Thompson." Backing out, I had to tell Mom, "This is not for us."

Finally, our driver casually sauntered up wearing nothing less than blue-and-white seersucker pants and a Hawaiian shirt. He pointed to our ride—a gold minivan. By then, we didn't care what it was. I said, "Good, let's go!"

If Mom hadn't been there to see this, I would've thought I was hallucinating. We were on our way in what I'm pretty sure was the world's only gold minivan covered with red-and-yellow floral Hawaiian carpeting, not just on the floor, but on the walls and ceiling too.

But soon, we were stuck. I knew, of course, that New York has traffic, but this was total gridlock. It didn't help that our driver seemed unsure of where he was taking us. I said, "Can you just get us close to Times Square?" As the minutes passed, Mom and I stopped talking, aware that if we didn't arrive soon, we could blow our chance. Pressure was mounting, and we didn't think about what would happen when we got to the studio. We were just hoping we'd get there.

The producer called again, wondering how close we were.

Hanging up, I leaned forward and said to the driver, "Can you please stop?"

He asked, "Here? Now?"

Deciding we'd be better off on foot, I said, "Yes, stop the car."

With that, on a hot July day crowded with tourists, Mom and I were running through Times Square, loaded down with shopping bags full of cookies. My feet were so sweaty that they were sloshing around in my shoes, and the clip in my hair was coming loose. It would've been easier to sit down, throw the cookies away, and forget the whole thing. But that's not us. We'd done some harebrained things, but this had to top them all. And the best part was, I didn't care.

I called out over my shoulder, "Mom, you okay?"

"I'm right behind you," she responded. "Keep going!"

Finally, we arrived at the correct address, but we couldn't find a way in. As we scurried up and down the sidewalk, I asked Mom, "How do you get into this place?"

I was about to text the producer to meet us outside when Mom peeked around the corner and said, "Susan, over here."

She pointed out a security guard in a black suit with an earpiece, who was blocking a concealed black door with a little sign: "Times Square: Stage Entrance." The guard barely glanced in our direction as we approached him; I can only imagine how ridiculous we must have looked. Then Mom said, "Excuse me, we're looking for Fifteen Hundred Broadway."

Gazing down at the two of us, he asked, "What are you looking for?"

I wanted to say, *Trust me, I don't believe this either.* But instead, I said, "We're here for David Muir."

He gave us a look that said, *Sure, ladies, you and everyone else.* I quickly mentioned the producer's name and showed his email, then the guard pointed to the door with a smile and said, "Security is inside."

The producer met us and took us up an elevator, we tied on our Susansnap aprons, and three minutes later, cameras were rolling as the producer said, "Let's keep it fresh. I like to get the initial greeting on camera." We weren't feeling too fresh, but we were ready.

Then in came David Muir. After the hellos, David said, "Persistence pays off. I liked your story from the first time you wrote. It kept getting put in the pile." That was either a great compliment or a very embarrassing moment.

Surprisingly, I wasn't nervous, and neither was Mom. After all, it was just the two of us sharing our story, what we do and why, with an interested guy. The interview was quick, and afterward, we had a casual off-camera conversation. David was gracious and kind, and I enjoyed our short time there. We got our picture taken with him, then we went back out the same concealed black door through which we'd entered and headed to Junior's, a deli we like, for BLTs and fries.

One of my favorite things to do in the city is walk. I love to see the people, the shops, the restaurants, the energy. You'll find all kinds of people doing all sorts of things, and that's what makes it such a great place. As we walked that day, I could have felt unimportant and insignificant, but I didn't. I remember thinking, *I feel fortunate that I am who I am. I love my story. I love what I know. I'd never give it back. And I'm grateful that I have the most amazing mom.*

We came across an old, beautiful Catholic church, St. Malachy's, nestled between a restaurant and a theater. We stopped in to say a quick thank-you and light a candle. I'm not sure if I've ever heard God talking to me, but he's heard me talking to him a lot along the way. He's done a lot for me, and I believe that one day I'll meet Aunt Sue.

As we continued our stroll, it dawned on me there was someone I was hoping to say hi to. We'd written back and forth a few times, because we had something in common: Hodgkin's. I tapped Mom's arm and said, "Hold up a second." Then I wrote a one-line email: "Are you by chance around for a quick hi?" The old Susan never would have done that. I hit Send. I checked my phone a few times, but there was no reply, and I thought, *No big deal.*

It had been a really good day, and Mom and I had gotten to experience it together. Mom flagged a taxi, and we were on our way back to the airport. It was a beautiful evening, with a breeze blowing through the partly open windows. There was traffic, but we were moving. I pulled my phone out to check my email again.

"Mom," I said, then waited until I had her full attention. "We got a book deal." I couldn't believe what I was saying. Of course, we'd been writing and working on this but didn't know where it would ever lead. Just when I thought that day couldn't get more unreal, it did.

We had arrived at the airport and were checking in at a Delta kiosk when I received a response to the email I'd sent hours earlier. Ethan Zohn had written me back. He's well known as the guy who won the third season of the show *Survivor*, but I knew him as the guy who had survived Hodgkin's. While our tickets were printing, I read that he was having an event in an hour, and he'd invited us to stop by.

I'd never had a chance to meet anyone who'd had my kind of cancer, let alone someone who was near my age and who made it seem okay. I wanted to meet Ethan so I could thank him in person. I wanted to thank him for me and for Aunt Sue. He had chosen to share his story publicly, even though he didn't have to, and he'd made a difference to me. I was vacillating: *What should we do? Our flight leaves at seven o'clock, and his event is at six.*

Seeing me, Mom asked, "What's wrong?"

"Nothing," I answered. "I just heard from Ethan. Don't laugh, but he's invited us to an event at six."

"I'm not laughing. Do you want to go?"

"Our flight leaves in an hour."

"I know, but let me go to the ticket counter. It won't hurt to ask." Mom knew that this meant something to me, and she began negotiating with the Delta employee.

After a few minutes, the employee pointed to me and asked, "It's you that had cancer?" I nodded. It turned out her mom had been a survivor for two years. She said, "That stuff is ugly." And just like that, she bumped our tickets back two hours.

We found ourselves running, once again, out to the airport taxi stand, and off we went to the event. We didn't have much time to get there, say hello, and get back to the airport. We weren't entirely sure where we were going, so Mom zipped into a random hotel and asked, "Where's the Core Club?" With some directions, we found the party and walked in. My heart was pounding for a bazillion reasons—the first one probably being that Mom and I looked like waiters standing in the corner of this chichi event. We were wearing the same jeans, golf shirts, sneakers, and aprons we'd worn to ABC that morning. I tried to catch Ethan's eye from the cocktail lounge, but it wasn't working. I chuckled at how outrageous this was. No one I knew would do this, but there we were.

Finally, there was a break, and the guests began mingling. Ethan spotted me and greeted me with arms wide open. Instantly, our conversation went to "insider cancer talk." I found myself feeling composed in a way that I hadn't before. Ethan was not just polite, but endearing, even asking about Aunt Sue. It was an uncommonly natural and nice moment.

It might sound surprising, but I realized that day that I liked winging it. In fact, I love to wing it now—whatever happens, happens.

Leaving the party, we'd walked two blocks when tears started streaming down my face. Mom asked, "Are you okay?"

I looked at Mom and threw my hands up. I didn't have words. I could not believe the day we'd just had.

That day was not supposed to happen, but it did. And I'm so glad I showed up.

Susansnaps continues to grow with more orders and new shoppers every day. Mom and I are grateful for every order and every customer that has walked through our door. After the "Made in America" piece aired, we got our largest single order to date: three thousand boxes of cookies for one company. It took four pallets and a forklift to ship that order. That was a sight I never thought I'd see.

I wake up thankful, grateful for each new day, wondering what it will bring. I sort of hate to admit it, but part of me likes the unknown now. If someone had told me even half of the things that were going to happen to me, I would have said, "Me? I don't think so. No, no thank you." But that's not how it works. I see each day as the possibilities it could hold. Anything is possible.

If you've ever felt like your burden is more than you can bear,

Mom and I are here to encourage you not to stop, but instead to persevere, because a better version of you may well be waiting on the other side. Life might not be perfect, but you can choose to be unsnappable.

Mom and I have instinctively relied on each other, and that made the tough times more bearable and the ridiculous times more fun. We've become sidekicks, pals, and partners in crime, doing things as awful as spending Fridays stuck in our chemo cubical, as funny as searching for the perfect wig, as hard as attending a long road show with no sales, and as exciting as sipping champagne alongside Martha Stewart.

It wasn't easy, and I had struggles. But despite all the pain, worry, and doubt, I wouldn't give it back. I gained a new perspective. I might not have always seen it this way, but I'm grateful, because I've learned and done things I never would have dreamed of when I was that eager college girl with the black suit. Together with Mom, I've survived a life-threatening illness, and I've created a specialty cookie company from the ground up. I've been zapped daily by radiation, and I've baked fourteen thousand gingersnaps in a day. I'm always aware of the fact that life can change in a snap. And when it does, I'll be okay. I know now that I'm stronger than I thought I was. I will muster up the courage and the strength to carry on. I've also learned to let go a little. There's no need to hold on so tightly.

When I was twenty-two years old, I couldn't have fathomed

that I'd be able to joke about the name Susan being cursed when I found out I had Hodgkin's, just like Aunt Sue. That the gingersnaps Mom baked in our garage as a pastime would turn into a business. That the same boyfriend who sat in a waiting room listening to a surgeon say *cancer* would eventually say, "Susan, will you marry me?" That having treatment alongside Dad would be oddly comforting. That I would find a way to smile every day at radiation, even though it was miserable and awkward. That Mom and I would have cramps in our hands after hand-scooping thirty thousand gingersnaps with a mini ice cream scoop. That we'd die laughing as we carried $6,000 into Waffle House because we didn't know where else to store the cash we'd made at a holiday gift show. Or that, like Aunt Sue, we would find a way to celebrate the good, the bad, and the mundane. Life is short. Go for it. Anything is possible.

I don't know what my life would've been like if I hadn't been diagnosed, and I don't care to. Mom says cancer made me fearless. My sister says I went from ordinary to extraordinary. I'm not sure about all that, but I do know I have an incredible story to share. One that I hope inspires you to carry on.

Dear Sue,

Shortly after you died, I was given cartons of materials from your years of teaching, in hopes that I could put them to good use. I was surprised to find one file filled with sheet music that we used to play on our guitars. You had used those songs to teach fifth and sixth graders in summer school. I was heartbroken looking through your work and missing you so much, when I turned over a blank sheet and saw your handwriting. It was a short list of party details that you'd jotted down for yourself. Nineteen words. It was for that bridal shower you threw for a friend.

As I looked closer, I gasped at the date. Although I shouldn't have been, I was amazed. There you were, thinking of others. You were celebrating a major life event for someone else, pouring yourself into the details, creating a party at your home, and making someone else happy. Doing something normal, blending into the everyday moments that all of our lives are made up of. Living. And you did it without so much as a word to anyone. Hardly anyone outside of our family and dearest friends knew you were sick. You hosted that bridal shower on Saturday, May 21, 1977. Fourteen days later, you were gone.

I've kept that scrap of paper in my dresser, and through the years, I've pulled it out countless times. When life got tough, you helped remind me to keep going. Because you lived, I learned to see things differently. You made me a different friend, wife, *mom, and daughter. Your generosity made me more generous, your kindness taught me to try to be more kind, your bravery made me more brave, and your strength made me strive to be stronger. I would come to need all those lessons you taught me as a young girl to be a better person when my family needed me. It would never be as hard for me, and I would never feel as hopeless because of the life you lived and the example you set for me. Remember when you used to tell me, "Laur, it doesn't matter"? You saw things your own way. And you know what? So does Susan. Not a week goes by that she doesn't echo the same thing: "Mom, it doesn't matter!"*

The day of your funeral, as I was sitting in the limousine, I took one last look out the window to see your casket covered in roses resting up on the hillside at the cemetery. I thought, So that's it? *You were here and now you were gone. I felt a crushing emptiness.* What am I going to do without you? *I had no choice but to lean on what Dad told me the day after you died. He said to me, "We have to find a way to go on, Laura. Life is for the living." No one knew that better than you. The limo started moving, and we pulled away.*

I knew I would never forget you, but I didn't know my own daughter, Susan, would get to know you—understand you—in a most unfathomable way. I ached for someone to feel your presence and understand not just who you were but what you were made of. What a price would be paid for my prayers to be heard. It was a couple of months after Susan's treatment when she asked me something about you. With all assuredness, Susan said to me, "You know, Mom, there are worse things than dying." She left me speechless.

And about your name on a cookie, I hope you don't mind! I knew I wanted to remember you... Who would have ever thought it'd go down like this? Thank you from the bottom of my heart for being you.

Love,
Laura

Epilogue

FOR YEARS AFTER I FINISHED TREATMENT, I HAD follow-up appointments with Dr. Weens. They became part of my routine, and I learned not to get too worked up or worried about them in advance. I assumed I'd always have to have them. But at the end of one appointment, Dr. Weens smiled at me as I hopped off the examination table. "I think we're all done here," she said.

"Okay," I said. "Bye, Dr. Weens. See you next time."

"No, Susan. You're all done." She smiled again, broader this time. "You don't have to come back anymore."

Relief washed over me as I stood in the exam room. I had longed to hear those words, but I never thought I would. Now the day had finally come. It was over—not just for me, but for Mom too. We had gotten through it together.

After I was pronounced officially cured, Randy and I wondered about having a family, although we weren't sure if it would be possible, after all the treatments I'd gone through at such a young age. When I got pregnant, we were thrilled and began preparing to start our lives as a family of three. But then, in the midst of writing chapters for this book, the scariest, most unlikely thing happened—I had my baby when I was only twenty-seven weeks pregnant (or three months before my due date). Either way you want to look at it, it was way too early.

That day, I was rushed to the hospital in terrible pain. After being monitored for a few hours, my baby's heart rate dropped quickly, and I was rushed into emergency surgery. I was terrified—but not for myself. *Give me surgery. Do what you have to do*, I thought. *What about the baby?* As I lay on the operating table with an anesthesiologist on each arm, working to put me out, I looked directly at my doctor and mouthed, "I am scared. I am so scared."

There was no time to walk me through what was happening. All I knew was that my baby was only twenty-seven weeks along, and that he had to come out *now*. I was panicking. It was too soon.

The next morning, twelve hours after the emergency C-section, it was time for me to go see our baby, who we named Nolan. Randy had been with him, but I hadn't seen him or touched him myself. Randy kept me calm and did an amazing job of holding it together. We'd just been thrown into this situation, and there wasn't time to think, *What are we going to do? How will we handle this?* We just did.

Randy and a nurse wheeled me to the Special Care Nursery (just a nicer name for the neonatal intensive care unit). Inside, it was dimly lit and very warm, with a few rows of incubators covered with blankets. This was not what Randy and I had pictured when we dreamed of having a baby. I'd never seen anything like this, and I was devastated.

As I looked into the clear plastic box where our son was sleeping, I saw an extremely tiny, yet beautiful baby boy. I stared at him and whispered, "Hi, baby. Oh my, you're doing such a good job. A really good job. I'm so proud of you. I'm right here, sweetie." I'd heard those words before. My mom's voice was coming through me. That was the same chant that Mom had repeated to me in the middle of the night, when she was lying on the floor next to my bed while I was going through chemo.

We were only allowed to stay with Nolan for a short time, and when I got back to my hospital room, I was overwhelmed with emotion. After seeing my son inside that incubator, I understood my mom in a new way. This must have been how she had felt when I was sick—heartbroken, worried, and helpless. I understood what it was like to be willing to do anything for your child.

I didn't get to hold Nolan for three days. I sat in a huge gliding armchair (sort of like an oversize vinyl recliner… Ring a bell?) next to Nolan's incubator to watch his nine o'clock feeding, which was essentially a few drops of milk through a feeding tube. I took off my sweatshirt, and the nurse moved my tiny, tiny little baby, with all these wires, monitors, and IVs, and placed him against my bare skin. She told me not to move my fingers against his thin, purplish skin, because it could rip.

When I finally held him, with the top of his head grazing my collarbone, my heart exploded. I was overwhelmed with love for this baby, and I was overcome with heartache because he had to fight so hard and I couldn't fix it for him. I put my head back against the chair, closed my eyes, and just cried. I had never felt something so incredible in my entire life. His tiny body was thumping up and down from the oxygen being pumped into him, and then, slowly, he moved his frail arm up and placed his hand on my collarbone. He held on to me. It was amazing and heartbreaking.

As I closed my eyes and felt his little arm reaching up and resting on me, I felt like he was letting me know, *I'm okay. I'm right here, Mom. See? Don't be sad. I'm here.* On the other hand, I also felt like he wanted to say, *Please help me. I don't want to do this.* It was just the way I had felt when I was sick—wanting to be strong and show Mom that I was okay, but also needing her to be there for me.

After a few minutes, the nurse put Nolan back in his incubator. He needed to rest, to grow, and to go back into his regulated environment. Randy said, "Suz, it's time to go. We'll come back tomorrow. Nolan needs to rest."

Nolan would grow stronger each day, but it was a long process. Day after day, Nolan had to work hard, to fight hard. It was terribly upsetting for me to watch him and see his determi-nation, his lively will, and also his sweet nature. Mom said, "He's a lot like someone else I know. I've seen this before. Tough and feisty, and the sweetest little thing."

Seventy-three days later, Nolan came home happy and healthy.

I think my son is like my dad and Aunt Sue, and I hope he is like me—faced with incredible challenges, never giving up, and trying to do it all with a smile. We're a family of fighters. We're unsnappable.

Acknowledgments

Dear Susan,

Writing this book has been as much a part of our story together as anything else we've done. I've watched you write as the months have gone by. Undeterred you kept going. We'd talk, laugh, and sometimes cry, and then you'd write some more. We'd get stuck morning, noon, and late into the night. You'd call to me from over our store desk, voice brimming with frustration, "Come on, Mom. What comes next? What's the next word?" Then, you'd put your head back down and start writing again, asking, "How does this sound?"

There were moments when I feared you wanted to quit, but I desperately hoped you wouldn't. And you didn't, you pushed yourself to write more and you pushed me to stay with it too. Thank you. I didn't want to let you down and with that I've relived some of my happiest and saddest moments. All along, I

*believed this was your story to tell. It just took some time to find
the right words. And you did.*

*Love,
Mom*

I was never into books as a kid. It's probably because reading wasn't my strong suit. My grandpa couldn't believe I didn't like reading, and the fact that Mom and I wrote our own book would blow him away! Honestly, I'm still not sure how we pulled it off either, but I am proud of the writing, the story telling, and our effort to share what we hope is even just a glimmer of inspiration. That's what kept me wanting to get this thing right. That hope that we could inspire even one reader.

We are grateful to those who have helped us along the way, but I must first say this book would not have happened without my mom. She was the steady voice saying "You can do this" when I doubted. I'll never forget our tears and uncontrollable laughter in writing *The Cookie Cure*. Mom, we did it!

There wouldn't be a book without our dedicated literary agent, Jo-Lynne Worley. The Worley-Shoemaker agency has stood by us from the beginning. Jo-Lynne and Joanie, thank you for believing in us and continually telling us to keep writing. A special thank you to the late Dr. Kathy Cramer for once telling us that someone would want to read what we have to say. To our editor, Anna Michels, thank you for your patience in working on this project with us. We are grateful for our publisher and the entire team at Sourcebooks.

It goes without saying that Aunt Sue has a special place in my heart. This certainly would have been a very different story without her, perhaps no story at all. If I could give all this back to meet her for five minutes, I would. But, that's not how it works. Aunt Sue—I am better for "knowing" you.

Dad, thank you for being adamant that I write what I know. You are the most supportive and caring father. Your selflessness doesn't go unnoticed. I have been blessed with wonderful parents and to be a part of a fun and loving family. To Robert, Luke, and Carey, I am lucky to call you, not only my siblings, but my friends. And Carey, where in the world would I be without you? You are priceless.

To Randy, I know you didn't really want your name in the book, and if so you wanted to be "Gustavo"…sorry! Thank you for not laughing when I said, "gingersnap company" years ago, and "writing a book" years later. Your love and confidence have pushed me to be the best version of myself. You and I are better because we're together. And to my sweet boy, Nolan. You are the pure joy in each day.

And from Mom:

Ken, your "it's not about me" attitude is unmatched. Not only did you protect the kids from your worries, I know you protected me too. I am grateful for you and each day we have together.

To my children, Robert, Susan, Luke, and Carey, I am proud of the caring people you have become. There is nothing better than listening to your hysterical banter around the table! I love being your mom. I hope you carry my aunt Sue stories with you always. Randy, I've witnessed your courage during life-shattering moments. You know you are an exceptional person to me. And Nolan, you are the most unexpected gift.

To my parents, Bob and Connie Carver, it is my good fortune to be your daughter. For Mother, who lived by the motto "I only knew to carry on." And Dad, for reminding me to "Lean on me. My shoulders are broad." I did, and thank you. To Chris and John, and your memories of the happy days we shared with Sue as the Carver kids. Also, I have a special thank you for Hoxsie for giving Sue so much joy and happiness. I am exceedingly grateful for our lasting friendship. And to Andrea for your generosity in making that possible. To my uncle, Don McNamee, for his own quiet courage and generous support.

Mom and I are grateful to our incredible friends. Thank you to Anastasia, Stephanie, Gracie, Ellen, Claire, Brenda, and Luanne for being the voices of encouragement along the way. We also feel grateful for our dear friend Sister Sally White, GNSH, for her every prayer.

I wish to especially acknowledge Dr. Joan Weens, MD, for her integral part in saving my life and my dad's. We are grateful for, not only her brilliance, but also her compassion. Thank you to the amazing doctors, nurses, and staff at Atlanta Cancer Care, St. Joseph's Hospital, and Emory. Dr. Michael Seyfried, MD, thank you for never being too busy for your patients.

To the cancer researchers and fundraising organizations—keep going. Your work makes a difference. We are acutely aware that every hour someone is hearing the words they never wanted to hear. Nothing about that is okay.

One last thing, there have been countless people cheering Mom and I along from the very beginning. Whether it was a kind word, comment, suggestion, phone call, email, interview, article, television segment, or photograph you have our sincere gratitude. You kept us going and helped get our cookie idea from garage to store to the nation, and even more so, you helped keep a cookie with a message of hope alive.

Thank you,
Susan

About
the Authors

Susan Stachler is a cancer survivor and cofounded Susansnaps with her mom, Laura Stachler. Susan graduated from Auburn University and lives in Atlanta with her husband and son. Laura graduated from the University of Southern California is the mother to four children and also resides in Atlanta with her husband, Ken. After surviving Hodgkin's lymphoma at age twenty-two, Susan joined her mother in her dessert business and began building their now nationally recognized cookie company, Susansnaps. Laura and Susan went from caregiver and patient to entrepreneurs and, through it all, mother and daughter. Their unique gingersnap cookie company, Susansnaps, is based in Atlanta, Georgia.